The Career Development Professional's Survival Guide

An A to Z

Jules Benton and Chris Targett

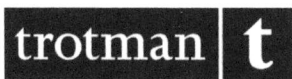

The Career Development Professional's Survival Guide

This first edition published in 2025 by Trotman, an imprint of Trotman Indigo Publishing Ltd, 18e Charles Street, Bath BA1 1HX.

© Trotman Indigo Publishing Ltd 2025

Authors: Jules Benton and Chris Targett

All illustrations by Jules Benton and Chris Targett.

British Library Cataloguing in Publication Data
A catalogue record for this book is available from the British Library.

Paperback ISBN 978-1-911724-67-4
eISBN 978-1-911724-68-1

All rights reserved. This book is sold subject to the condition that it shall not, by way of trade or otherwise, be lent, resold, hired out or otherwise circulated without the publisher's prior written consent in any form of binding or cover other than that in which it is published and without a similar condition including this condition being imposed on the subsequent purchaser. No part of this publication may be reproduced, stored in a retrieval system or transmitted in any form or by any means, electronic and mechanical, photocopying, recording or otherwise without prior permission of Trotman Indigo Publishing.

Every effort has been made to trace copyright holders and to obtain their permission for the use of copyright material. The publisher apologises for any errors or omissions, and would be grateful to be notified of any corrections that should be incorporated in future editions of this book.

The authorised representative in the EEA is Easy Access System Europe Oü (EAS), Mustamäe tee 50, 10621 Tallinn, Estonia.

Printed and bound in the UK by CMP Ltd.

 All details in this book were correct at the time of going to press. To keep up to date with all the latest news and updates and to access the online resources that accompany this book, use this QR code or visit **www.trotman.co.uk/pages/the-career-development-professionals-survival-guide-resources**

Contents

About the authors	**vii**
Foreword	**ix**
A big hello	**xi**
Acknowledgements	**xiii**

A   1

   Alphabet soup? – an abundance of abbreviations or acronyms   1

B   2

   Beginnings – things to consider when starting in a new role, a different setting or a new job   2
   Body doubling – a technique where you work alongside another person, either physically or virtually, to enhance focus and motivation   6

C   8

   Communication – *the single biggest problem in communication is the illusion that it has taken place* ~George Bernard Shaw   8
   Complaints – don't panic! Listen and learn   12
   Continuous Professional Development (CPD) – occupational and educational knowledge   16
   Curiosity – indulge your own curiosity by finding out how others work   22

D   24

   Decisions – what affects decision making   24
   Designing your day – some of the ways you can structure a day's careers interactions   29
   Difficult conversations – *careers work doesn't really matter or isn't important; You must do shorter career sessions; You need to fill up our sixth form or local college; There's no point in 'inclusive approaches'; You can't have a room; Clients who say 'I dunno' or 'I don't know'*   38
   Disabled – you have rights   46
   Disclosure and barring – what the different kinds of checks are, and who needs them   48

E — 50

Emails – top tips for helping to ensure that emails don't clog up your life — 50
Equality and equity – what they mean and why they matter — 52
Ethics – ethical use of different social media and technology platforms; Unethical Practice; Agendafication — 53
Everyone has a right to career guidance – just saying! — 61

F — 62

Find your tribe – why we need our own circles of support — 62
Future gazing – what will happen next in the careers sphere? — 69

G — 71

Going places – things to remember the first time you go to a setting — 71

H — 73

Have a go! – how Chris and Jules got over their own anxieties and learnt to embrace things outside their comfort zones — 73
Humour – when is a joke not a joke? — 76

I — 77

Information sharing – what should we share, and how? — 77

J — 83

Just one thing – why doing 'just one thing' can be so powerful — 83

K — 84

Kindness – ways of being, which we can consider to improve our lot — 84

L — 87

Learning styles – are they a myth? — 87
Looking after the planet – musings on sustainable practice — 90

M — 93

Magic – why Terry Pratchett could have been writing about us — 93
Mistakes – what we've learnt from ours — 94

N — 96

No such thing as a silly question – a bit about different kinds of questions and how they can be used — 96

O — 103

Opportunities – activities which promote the development of self-awareness; various ways of researching opportunities — 103

P — 107

Personalising action plans – what is the purpose of our action plans? — 107
Philosophy and careers – a romp through some thinkers — 109
Play – why is it important? — 115

Q — 116

Quick or slow – how to slow down . . . or stop — 116

R — 120

Realism – mental capacity and 'unwise' choices — 120
Reflection – how and why to reflect on your work — 122
Refreshments – the art and etiquette of food and drink — 124

S — 127

Sick and tired – is a change as good as a rest? — 127
Social media – for business, for/with clients, for ourselves and for CPD — 130
Staying safe – a few thoughts on how and why this is so important — 135

T — 138

Transitions – techniques which support our clients to 'move' — 138

U — 141

Unconditional positive regard – what to do when accepting and respecting others as they are gets hard — 141

V — 145

Visibility – why should we make ourselves 'seen' — 145

W — 146

What should I wear? – some personal musings on dress codes and appearance — 146

X — 152

X-rated – sometimes clients talk about inappropriate things! — 152

Y — 154
Yet – the power of yet and growth mindset — 154

Z — 155
Zenith – 'the time at which something is most powerful or successful' – what we might call Impact! — 155

Zero tolerance? – if a client is unaware they are doing something wrong (and it is not harmful, or an immediate threat) should we adopt a policy of zero tolerance? — 156

The Zone – 'a region or area set off as distinct from surrounding or adjoining parts'. So, this is the section without our usual chit-chat – just loads of explainers and links to things we think you'll find useful and interesting — 158

About the authors

Chris Targett

Chris Targett is a dynamic and innovative Careers Adviser who received the CDI's 'UK Careers Adviser of the Year' Award in 2021. His background in art and philosophy informs his creative approach, supporting young people, schools and colleagues across the guidance community. Chris currently works as an Area Manager and Careers Adviser for the charity CXK, and he is also Chair of the Careers Writers Association (CWA).

Jules Benton

Jules Benton has over 35 years' experience working as a Careers Guidance Professional, Trainer and Consultant. She specialises in careers guidance for individuals who are disabled, have learning support needs or experience other barriers to inclusion. Jules is also Chief Executive of Cosmic Cactus, a service that provides support for transitions to employment, training and education.

Foreword

I still remember my first few months as I entered the career development profession in 2008, when I joined the UK Government-funded Connexions service. As excited as I was at the prospect of what was (then) a thriving, holistic, advice and guidance service for young people, I also remember a sense of trepidation. How would I be trained to help often vulnerable young people, professionally and effectively? What knowledge would I need to build in order to help me do my job effectively? Where would I turn if (inevitably) I found myself facing an unfamiliar challenge, or if I made a mistake?

Fortunately for me, I was surrounded by many more experienced professionals who were usually happy to help me tackle these challenges and grow as a professional, as well as a well-established framework of formal training and professional development. In today's career development landscape – at least in England – the rich array of support that I was able to enjoy is unfortunately no longer available for many new entrants to the profession. Hence, the importance of the book you now hold. Jules Benton and Chris Targett have produced what I can only describe as an essential part of a new career development professional's initial training, addressing aspects of the work that go beyond the factors that are explicitly addressed by the formal qualifications currently available.

Organised as an 'A-Z' of factors that new career development professionals almost certainly will encounter in their first year or so of their career, this book covers a surprisingly wide range of situations, from dress codes, to mistakes, to social media. Throughout, Jules and Chris offer wise, compassionate advice, making this book a helpful companion accompanying the reader's first, tentative steps in their journey as a Careers Professional. Experienced professionals will still find much profit in reading this book, as it offers a helpful reminder of how to tackle a multitude of professional dilemmas that can be encountered even with years of experience.

The landscape of career development training and professional development has changed radically since I first entered the profession 17 years ago, but many of the challenges facing careers professionals remain. This book fills a much-needed gap in the tapestry of support that all new entrants to the profession need, and as such I have no hesitation in recommending it.

Dr Oliver Jenkin PGCE RCDP, NICEC Fellow.
CDI Senior Professional Development and Standards Manager,
and Editor of the CDI's magazine, Career Matters.
September 2025

A big hello

Hello!

We are delighted you've chosen to read our second book.

This A to Z guide came out of discussions we had about what we didn't have room for in the previous book – including the things we both see are overlooked in the current climate of time-poor contracts and lack of capacity within the sector.

As with the previous book, this will be a mixture of both our voices. We intend it to be friendly and informative, aimed at both the newly qualified Career Development Professional (CDP) wandering out into the wilds of the careers sphere, as well as the more experienced professional looking to change roles, improve their practice or pick up some top tips to make working life easier.

We've put in the things that you may not be taught now while training to be a CDP or starting a new role. The kinds of conversation that used to take place around the water cooler, or in the office kitchen. All the bits and pieces of information that a comprehensive induction would cover. We are very aware that these opportunities have been reduced, or have even disappeared, in recent times.

We'd like to share with you the things that keep us nurtured and joyous in our work. It is intended as a light-hearted but pragmatic guide. We have woven in some bits and pieces of theory along the way, and some questions that we ask ourselves and each other. There is a *Zone* at the end with a list of explainers and links. The information listed in the *Zone* can also be found in the online resources that accompany this book. To access, scan the QR code or visit the website address given at the start of this book.

This book is a mixture of lived experience, observation and reflection. Take what works for you and discard what doesn't . . . it is a guide for you to dip in and out, not a manual.

Our aim is that it makes your life easier in your daily practice and helps you carve out space to love your work and day-to-day being.

We hope you find it useful and a fun read!

Acknowledgements

A big thank you to everyone who bought our last book, *Career Development and Inclusive Practice*. We really appreciate the support and love the book has garnered. You sharing in our enthusiasm means the world to us.

Massive thanks to our families and friends, as always, for their support and belief in our endeavours.

This book wouldn't have been possible without the wisdom shared by many colleagues over the years, past and present; thank you to all of you. We have referenced a few of you within the book, but there are so many people out there who we have learnt from that we couldn't fit everyone in!

And always the best teachers . . . our clients.

A few key people who have been game changers for us:

Vicki, Roberta and Malcolm, who have been continuous guiding lights over the years for Chris (as well as great dining companions). And Sarah, his manager, who has done so much to mentor Chris in his development as a manager of the young people's careers service at CXK.

Liane and Olly for their insight, patience and encouragement – Jules finds them both inspiring and would never have written a book without their support.

Last, but absolutely crucially, Alexandra (from Trotman) who has enabled us to be authors and enjoy it!

Thank you all.

A

Alphabet soup?

Alphabet soup is a metaphor for an abundance of abbreviations or acronyms.

The careers sphere is littered with abbreviations, initialisms and acronyms! As we work our way through the alphabet, we'll add in explainers for some of these. There is also a list of terms commonly used within careers, and learning support, in the *Zone* at the end of this book

With reference to our own jobs, we are mostly going to use the terms *Career Development Professional (CDP)* and *Career Practitioners* in this guide.

Career development professionals specialise, and are professionally qualified, in helping individuals navigate their career paths, make informed decisions and develop strategies to achieve their career goals.

Those providing career development support (career practitioners) may be called careers assistants, careers advisers, careers leaders, careers coaches, career counsellors, careers consultants, career development experts, employability coaches and many more job titles.

Some of the examples will refer to *Advisers* or *Coaches* where this is the term used by the people who shared their thoughts with us.

 Insider tip

It is very confusing when people use so many different words and initials. Don't be afraid to ask for clarification.

B

Beginnings

The beginning is always today.

– Mary Wollstonecraft Shelley

Things to consider when starting in a new role, a different setting or a new job:

It's usual to feel nervous starting a new job. There are a bunch of things that can seem a bit overwhelming at the beginning.

- It's unfamiliar

New jobs involve new surroundings, responsibilities and social interactions.

- Are we good enough?

We get worried about meeting expectations, proving ourselves and doing new things. Feeling like a fraud or fearing being 'found out' as inexperienced (often called Imposter Syndrome) can contribute to anxiety.

- There are new people.

We are building new relationships with colleagues and experiencing a new organisational culture.

Change generally causes some anxiety.

We hope that if you feel like you need a bit of advice, a place to start your thought process, or just a familiar voice for reassurance, you can open up our book and find that safe place to begin from.

CDPs and practitioners work in a wide range of settings, including:

- Education;
- Careers services/offices;
- Community venues;
- Online;
- Telephone;
- People's homes;
- Prisons;
- Hospitals.

There are things which can make your working life much safer, healthier and easier.

One of these is having clear day-to-day systems and processes which enable you to deliver an effective service.

Arrangements around these will vary depending on who you work for:

- an independent organisation;
- employed directly by an education institution;
- self-employed;
- Local Authority, health service or Central Government.

Ensuring your foundations are taken care of before you start delivering your services will reduce the chances of misunderstandings and issues arising between you and the commissioner of your services, as well as enable you to deliver a better service for your clients.

This is a list of the common questions we would ask before starting delivery.

> Note: these questions don't replace the Risk Assessments the setting or organisation you work for require; and some questions apply to specific types of setting.

- What are your health and welfare arrangements for staff and for clients?
- What time should I be on site?
- What are the parking arrangements?
- Who is my day-to-day contact for the sessions and safeguarding?
- When is the end of the day for staff and for clients?
- Are there safeguarding arrangements in place that I need to be aware of, such as automatic locking rooms, keypads or fobs?

- When will clients be ready to start?
- How will we be arranging my working day?
- How many sessions would you like delivered across the day?
- Is there an option to run a drop-in session?
- Can I use outside space if this is appropriate?
- Is there time to talk through any actions required, or concerns, at the end of the day?
- Is there access to Wi-Fi?
- What is the room setup?
- Will there be a Teaching Assistant (TA) or Communication Support Worker available for students who want support?
- Are parents/carers invited to attend?
- Is there an option for virtual appointments? If so, what are the arrangements? Do clients know how to use the technology, or will they need support?
- How much time is provided for administration?
- What administration is required by the organisation I work for? Is there other admin required by the setting?
- When and where does the administration get completed?
- Are pen profiles provided before seeing clients? How and when can I access these? Are they written <u>with</u> the client?
- What do the pen profiles have on them? Risk assessments? Preferred communication methods? What is important to/for the client?
- What pre-session information can I send to clients? Is it possible to see clients prior to careers appointments to introduce myself, outline expectations and reduce anxiety?
- How/when do clients get told the time and location of their appointment with me?
- If the client has any questions or concerns before the session, how can they contact me?
- What format are action plans to be in? How creative and flexible can I be within these guidelines?
- Who are action plans shared with? What is the process for this and is it compliant with the latest data protection legislation?
- How does the careers guidance link with transition support, work-readiness or pastoral arrangements? (including other support staff or services who may be involved)

This isn't a definitive list – just a few questions to get you thinking about what you feel you may need in order to deliver an effective service; you may have other key questions that you would ask, and some of the above questions may not be as relevant for you in your setting. Write down all your questions before you are due to begin somewhere new and arrange a meeting with key personnel to give you an opportunity to ask them any questions you may have and iron out any issues.

We'll consider some of these questions – and the answers you may encounter – in a bit more depth over the following chapters.

 Insider tip

It takes a whole year to understand a setting.

Body doubling

For people with ADHD, and many of us with no label, the tasks we find more tedious can be stress-inducing.

For Chris . . . these are things that his 'interest-based nervous system' doesn't get a kick (or dopamine hit) from. Generally, spreadsheets, editing (Jules added this one to his list!) and doing his expenses.

Different people find different things motivating.

One of Chris' friends with ADHD loves a spreadsheet and finds them great. It is worth keeping this in mind when considering support strategies (different people need different things – and appropriate support is not impairment-based).

Body doubling is a technique for helping people focus on tasks which they find challenging to complete. It has gained popularity in ADHD forums online over the last few years. The technique involves those with ADHD working on their own tasks alongside others who are also working. It doesn't require the body double doing any of the ADHDer's work; rather, they just work steadily on their own tasks.

There are different theories as to why body doubling helps ADHDers. One is that it provides a model to mimic or copy, which provides the motivation. Many ADHDers have said how much of an impact the technique has had on their wellbeing and productivity. Those who don't have ADHD can also find body doubling useful as a motivating aid.

For Chris, he made the connection with body doubling after the Covid pandemic, whereby he actively chose to return to working at his head office in Ashford when faced with paperwork he found a challenge. Working at home on his own was challenging and resulted in Chris avoiding the tasks which didn't resonate with him, thereby increasing his levels of stress and impacting his mental health.

You may have to tweak the approach to ensure it works for you.

For example, Chris found that if he went into the office on a busy day he would just get distracted by people and not get as much work done as he wanted (defeating the object of the exercise). However, if he went in on a Friday, generally the office was a lot quieter and he could find himself working alongside others who were also working.

The other aspect of body doubling that can help is setting a few boundaries, such as:

- Talking and working – some people can happily chat while they work, others find it really distracting. If you have more than one room in the office, it is quite easy to set up a 'quiet room'. If there is only one space, maybe a 'quiet day' would work.
- When do coffee breaks happen? Finding someone whose rhythm you can get into sync with can really help. So, if there is not a set rule, you may want to sync with a coffee buddy.

For those of us without access to an office, setting up a video call where you can see someone else working can be a way to body double; as body doubling can be achieved virtually. There are even websites such as *Focus Mate* – follow the link in the *Zone* at the end – which are dedicated body doubling platforms to help aid productivity.

We hold a virtual office every Wednesday at Trotman – and I love it! I'd never realised this was a form of body doubling – it's very motivating.
– *Alexandra Price, Trotman*

Alternatively, if you are in school and doing paperwork at the end of the day after the career sessions, working in a classroom alongside a teacher marking or in the staff room with others who are working can be a way to body double.

C

Communication

The single biggest problem in communication is the illusion that it has taken place.
— George Bernard Shaw

We covered a lot about communication in our first book – *Career Development and Inclusive Practice* – so we aren't going to repeat what we wrote there.

Instead, we just want to get you thinking about some of the things we all say and do (almost without thinking) which are unhelpful, and some of the things that can really help when someone can't say what they want to.

When you are checking to see if you have communicated effectively instead of asking a closed question like 'does that make sense?' use your guidance techniques... get a client to explain what they think you've said in their own words.

Asking the question 'was that clear?' (even though we all do it almost unconsciously) has no outcome – if they say yes, we still don't know if they really understood, and if they say no, we have to ask another question to find out why!

As careers practitioners, most of us are pretty comfortable with spoken language. Many people are less comfortable. And some people (for example, those with sensory impairments, learning difficulties, anxiety or expressive language challenges) may find it really difficult to talk to you at all in words you understand. Other methods of communication are available – pictures, writing, assistive technology, construction or metaphorical tools, messaging, email, interpreters, advocates... to name but a few.

One of the biggest learning curves as a careers practitioner is understanding that what we think clients say and what they mean are two very different things!

Here are some classics that we have experienced over the years:

- 'Barista'... they meant Barrister. Lots of words sound similar.
- Engineer... they meant Motor Vehicle Technician (Mechanic).
- Astrologer... Astronomer.
- Go soliciting! There was a sensitive discussion about what this means... (it doesn't mean being a Solicitor!).

One of Chris' favourite ways to check for understanding is to ask clients to 'Paint me a picture of what you have in your head... don't worry about the "correct" career terms or job titles... what do you see yourself doing?'

This is just one of many ways to unlock what clients mean, to get an accurate idea of the thoughts in their heads.

And even without words it can get confusing. Jules thought a young person was trying to show her what they 'loved' – they were after all making a heart symbol with their hands and pointing to their heart. Turns out they were trying to convey they'd had a heart operation.

Checking in with clients from the outset (with sensitivity) what they actually mean is vital!

For when people can't speak...

Make sure to tell people you don't expect them to speak to you if they can't or don't feel comfortable to.

There is some excellent assistive tech around! We have put just a few examples below. There are links in the *Zone* at the end of the book.

Apple text-to-speech features:

- iPad/iPhone has a built-in text-to-speech facility (Speak Selection, accessed through Settings – General – Accessibility – Speech), which is excellent for reading short passages of text from the screen. For this young person, it would probably work best in conjunction with the Notes app, which includes a Speak Sentence option; otherwise, it can be a little fiddly to select text to be spoken.
- Speak Speech Synthesiser is a free app that allows the user to type, store and read back sentences. They can be simple 'chat' sentences, for example, 'How are you today?', 'Did you see Game of Thrones last night?', 'I liked the bit where...', and so on. The one drawback of the app is that every time you speak a sentence it is saved again, so you can easily end up with lots of copies of 'How are you today?'

- Ginger Writer 4+ Grammar Checker allows you to take part in unprepared chat, typing with word prediction to increase speed if typing is slow and a simple button to read the text out.
- Emergency Chat is a free app that can be used in situations where communication has broken down – it could be used to explain to a communication partner why you have difficulty speaking, so they will be patient and understanding.
- Siri is the iPad/iPhone's built-in speech recognition system. Most people use it for asking questions, finding directions and so on, but it can also be used for generating text.

Microsoft 365 text-to-speech features:

- Read Aloud is available in Word, Outlook, PowerPoint and OneNote. It reads the entire document or selected text aloud, with options to adjust the voice and reading speed.
- Speak is also built into Word, Outlook, PowerPoint and OneNote and reads aloud only the selected text.
- Immersive Reader can be found in Microsoft Edge and Office applications. Immersive Reader includes a Read Aloud feature that highlights text as it's read aloud.
- Dictate is available in Microsoft 365 and allows users to use speech-to-text to author content.

Many others are available.

Other (less techy) tools:

- Mini whiteboards: A mini whiteboard allows individuals to write down responses, providing a way to communicate without speaking.
- Recorded messages: Using recorded messages can be easier for some individuals to communicate than direct talking. Equally, some clients may prefer a recording of your session to a written record.
- Play (this has a section of its own).
- Professional support: Interpreters, speech and language therapists and so on. Check what support is available to clients in your settings and make a point of connecting with those people.

Communication

 Insider tips

Speech and language are complex! Don't expect people to be as comfortable with them as we are; and we still get a lot wrong! Not to worry . . . the first 2,000 one-to-one sessions are the trickiest (as we have a limited frame of reference).

Don't be afraid to advocate for your clients but, if you do, ask yourself first . . . are you doing so for your own reasons (to try and 'save them') or because they genuinely can't advocate for themselves? Leave the superhero pants at home!

Ensure you listen to your client to discover what their bottom line is and what their ideal position is before rushing into any advocacy. Always get their permission to advocate before you do so (being clear on what the boundaries and limits are to what you can do). And specifically state that you are advocating for them – saying what they want said, not giving your own opinion.

We talked in more depth about communication in our book *Career Development and Inclusive Practice*. If you'd like to read more, follow the link in the *Zone*.

Complaints

Try not to fear complaints – they are incredibly useful, and sometimes the only way that clients (or their circles of support) can be heard.

If you receive the complaint directly, try using some of the following responses:

- Start with a greeting and thank the complainant for bringing the issue to your attention.
- Acknowledge their complaint and show you understand their perspective and feelings.
- If they have not put their complaint in writing, ask if they would like to, or if they would prefer you to write down what they say.
- Write down the exact words the complainant uses and any responses you make.
- Use empathetic language to show you care about their experience.
- Offer an apology for any inconvenience or mistakes. This is NOT admitting you have done something wrong . . . simply that the miscommunication has been inconvenient and/or unhelpful.
- Avoid generic or automated apologies – make it sound genuine.
- Take responsibility for the issue without blaming the customer or external factors. Tell your complainant that you absolutely want the best service for everyone and are keen to improve anything that didn't seem useful.
- Explain the steps you are taking to resolve the issue and prevent it from happening again.
- Be specific about the actions you will take. For example, if you are referring the complaint to someone else, who else you will speak to, how you will contact them with your findings, and when?
- Offer a solution or compensation if appropriate.
- Thank them again for their patience and understanding.
- Provide follow-up information within the timeframe you agreed.
- Reiterate your commitment to resolving the issue.

Complaints are a great way of improving customer service!

In many organisations there are processes for dealing with complaints, where the complaint is picked up by someone not directly involved (someone independent); often the line manager of the person involved. These processes are there to protect all parties from the respondent through to the complainant.

Most organisations have a clear process for customers and clients to make a complaint, alongside processes which support freedom of information requests, which may form part of a complaint.

Being aware of the complaint procedures in your organisation, before a complaint happens, is important to protect yourself and your clients.

If you work for yourself (like Jules), make sure you have people you can turn to if you receive a complaint – this could include an independent HR company to deal with the complaint and a trusted colleague to talk the complaint through with before responding.

In most cases, depending on what the complaint is about, members of the public have recourse to take complaints to the professional bodies representing the individual (such as AGCAS or the CDI) as well as the organisation they work for. How each body or organisation would deal with this may vary.

> CDI: All CDI members should be concerned with the maintenance of good practice within the profession and must commit themselves to the CDI Code of Ethics which sets out the standards of professional conduct to which members must adhere.
>
> AGCAS: It is hoped that problems will normally be dealt with informally, in a spirit of conciliation without the need for recourse to a formal procedure. As a first step, if you do have any concerns regarding an AGCAS member's adherence to its Code of Ethics, this should be raised with the AGCAS Membership Manager in a courteous and constructive manner. If the response to the informal complaint or concern is unsatisfactory, you should use the formal process. You should only use the formal procedure if you consider that the concern or complaint is too serious to be dealt with informally or you are dissatisfied with the results of informal discussions.
>
> You can find the procedures which will be applied to deal with any complaints on their websites – links in the *Zone*.

There are, of course, complaints which can be made that relate to serious safeguarding or child protection allegations involving the police and the criminal justice system.

Taking suitable legal advice in such cases is essential, and our overview here doesn't explore this, but we need to recognise that such complaints can and do happen.

By the very nature of our work, we are vulnerable to false accusations and similar; we need to be mindful to protect ourselves and those we work with.

Simple things when setting up delivery, such as ensuring we deliver in rooms which have windows and are in public places so people can see what is going on, can keep us and clients safe from allegations.

It may be us making the complaint, or whistleblowing, to protect a client or to challenge unfair and/or illegal processes.

We know from child protection training that those wishing to abuse or prey on young people will try and get jobs in services and roles which support them. Therefore, it is our duty to remain vigilant and understand the policies and procedures which relate to this.

As career professionals, we walk the line between providers, parents/carers, clients, teachers, other practitioners and sometimes even our own employers. There is a good chance that at some point we are going to annoy someone or accidentally make a misstep or mistake. However it happens, at some point we will drop the ball.

For some of us, making a mistake is like water off a duck's back; it doesn't dent our sense of self at all. For others, especially those with neurodivergent brains who experience RSD (Rejection Sensitivity Dysphoria), it can feel devastating, leaving us replaying incidents in our mind months, if not years later. Often, the devastation we feel isn't congruent to the incident, as we overreact emotionally. We struggle to shake things off and have to use all our powers of logic and insights from counselling or therapeutic interventions which we may have received to battle with the sense of despair, so it doesn't eat us up. Sensitive and effective supervision can also help us contextualise missteps in our practice.

Many people with RSD and similar conditions also struggle with Imposter Syndrome, while also being prodigious overachievers. Trying to not fail or make any mistakes at all feels better than facing the emotional pit which comes from making a mistake and seemingly failing. We've put a couple of links in the *Zone* to some conversations about Imposter Syndrome.

Learning to live with mistakes and failure is in itself a life skill – one which can be hard won for some of us. We have covered a bit about developing a growth mindset in other sections.

- Chris has battled with RSD for years. It is only since his diagnosis of ADHD that he has been able to put a name to it. Being able to name it has enabled him to face it and understand it.
- We have used Chris' experience with RSD as an illustration of how being uniquely you can bring challenges that others may not understand. We all have our own issues – try to remind yourself of this when you struggle with a response from a client or colleague which you find puzzling, annoying or upsetting.

- For anyone wanting to know a bit more about RSD we've put a couple of links in the *Zone*.

What strategies can we use to deal with complaints?

We've covered the practical bits at the start of this section. But what about the emotional impact?

In most cases, to try and dissemble and/or hide a mistake will make things worse in the long term. If you've made a mistake and are aware of it, fess up and work with your employer, or those involved, to resolve it. In most cases, things are not insurmountable and most mistakes can be fixed.

When a complaint doesn't feel justified, this can sometimes be harder, as we wish to defend ourselves. It can get emotional and heated if we are not careful. Much like with responding to emails, taking a step back and allowing some time can be useful.

Beyond the due processes and recourse, there is emotional fallout from complaints, for all involved. How we react and feel in the long term can feel challenging, depending on what has happened and how it has been handled.

In a worst-case scenario, we may wish to walk away from the sector and have nothing more to do with it. It may be that we wish to change employer or we are worried about losing face or the respect of others.

Our reputation may be damaged, and we may feel bruised or emotionally worn out by the situation.

Taking steps to look after ourselves and our mental wellbeing is important, whether that is via emotional and counselling services, independent services or line management support and supervision.

We have put some things you might want to consider doing for yourself in our section on *Kindness*.

Part of being able to look after ourselves is undertaking the required training on a regular basis around working safely and ensuring we are up to date on courses and practices relating to General Data Protection Regulation (GDPR), Safeguarding and the Prevent duty. Many of our venues ask for evidence we are up to date, as do the providers of our public liability insurance.

Have a look at the *Staying Safe* section for a bit more on this.

Continuous Professional Development (CPD)

Why is CPD so important in career development work?

Occupational and educational knowledge

There has been a trend within careers work to focus on the decision-making and counselling aspects of the sector, which in itself isn't a bad thing. However, there is a danger in focusing on this, and the psychology behind how we make decisions, to the detriment of other aspects.

Careers is an interdisciplinary profession which draws from economics and sociology through to psychology and philosophy. There is a risk that we lose occupational knowledge if we focus too much on these. There is an illusion that the aim of building this knowledge is to turn CDPs into walking search engines (or encyclopedias, if you'd like an old school analogy). The reality couldn't be further from the truth.

We know that there is a danger in learning information by rote, as it can change so quickly and become out of date. It doesn't mean that learning occupational or educational knowledge is meaningless.

Learning occupational and educational knowledge is important for several key reasons:

- It helps us to understand terminology and concepts, how they relate to each other and affect the life chances of those we work.
- It helps us understand how different sectors relate and intersect with each other.
- It enables us to parse information and identify reliable and valid sources which can benefit our clients. Knowing where and how to find information is the skill we are aiming to develop.
- Occupational visits to education providers and employers help us to stay current and discover the 'exceptions to the rule' which can't be found in prospectuses or occupational profiles. They provide us with 'real' stories that we can use with clients (especially as part of a narrative approach which uses stories as a way to inspire).
- Undertaking research and producing our own occupational studies enables us to practice taking complicated, and sometimes contradictory, information and turning this into digestible and easier-to-use intelligence. Research can help us to get to the truth of a matter when initial searches are inconclusive or confusing.
- Our understanding helps us to support clients in interpreting information and making sense of possibilities.

To not build a personal working framework of understanding is to leave us being less effective and not as helpful to our clients as we can be.

> **Authors' note**
>
> Chris recently had a client who was trying to find out whether they could still study medicine with a low grade in Chemistry GCSE (which had been sat in Year 10). The local sixth form that provided A levels was reluctant to offer them Chemistry A level – worried that they lacked the underpinning core knowledge. The college offered Humanities A level.
>
> The client had arrived in the UK only a few years earlier, due to conflicts abroad, and Chris wanted to know whether extenuating circumstances could apply for them to access Higher Education and medicine. Was there a possible path available to them?
>
> In none of the available literature online or in books was there clarity.
>
> Chris used some of his time in the school where he was working to undertake research over several weeks (with the school's blessing). He contacted admissions tutors at universities across the country and discussed contextual offers, foundation year 0s, as well as other possible pathways.
>
> This led to identifying several possible pathways (depending on how their ability develops), including taking BTECs in Science to build knowledge to the appropriate level, followed by either a Biochemistry degree (or similar) with a foundation year 0, to provide access to graduate entry medicine later.
>
> Or they could take a path to the Allied Professions or Nursing and then later a medicine degree apprenticeship (or detour for a role as a Physician Associate).
>
> Without the underpinning occupational and educational knowledge, Chris wouldn't have been as effective in helping his client make sense of what was possible.

Many years ago the legendary Andy Gardner (who co-authored *The Higher Education Advisers' Handbook*) was delivering a keynote at a conference Chris attended. The key takeaways for Chris were to *never assume what is or isn't possible* and *do your research!*

It has formed a foundation of his approach to CPD within the sector.

It was one of the best pieces of advice he was ever given.

And one of Jules' favourite phrases is 'don't assume'.

Working practices around research are key when we consider the importance of checking the validity of information.

An observation we've shared, in a world where we have AI-driven search engines, is that strange and bizarre information is being dredged from the depths of the world wide web. Long forgotten and confusing nuggets of information, such as addresses of long-defunct professional organisations, through to qualifications that stopped running many moons ago.

It's more important than ever that career professionals lean into their training on how to research and consider the core fundamentals:

- Use more than one source for research.
- Compare and contrast sources.
- Check validity of information – why was the information collected, when and for what purpose?
- Where might there be inherent bias?
- If collected long ago, might it be out of date?

Occupational and pathway awareness

When we first started in careers, researching and undertaking occupational studies was a core requirement for training. It formed a robust foundation to develop careers practice on and still does (alongside the wider training on models and theories around decision-making and economics).

Some commentators ask, what's the point? It can all be found online anyway ... we don't need to know all the information or be a walking search engine ... so why bother?

There is a balance here to consider. It is impossible to understand the minutiae of every occupation and pathway; however, an understanding of occupations, educational and training pathways is part of the context within which we practise. To not develop a broad understanding is to have a diminished awareness of the world around us and our clients.

This includes having a reduced understanding of the possibilities and potential available to our clients. We need an awareness of how all the puzzle pieces fit together, so we can spot inaccuracies in the information available to us (and them) to make sense of where information may contradict or not be clear or accurate.

Through discussion we have been exploring the disparities in information being pulled through on some AI searches. Inaccurate information regarding qualifications from other countries, and qualifications that used to run in the UK but were cut many years ago, have been appearing.

Having an awareness of the accuracy and validity of what is written is vital. Using multiple sources helps us to check for accuracy. Having a good understanding of how to explore, use information and look for bias is part of our critical toolkit. We neglect keeping it up to date at our peril.

Knowing where to look for, and find, the information we need to support our clients is just as vital as being able to check its authenticity.

> **Authors' note**
>
> Chris and Jules have both recently worked with clients in Year 11 who were worried about going to college and had decided not to consider this as an option.
>
> Chris' client was worried about having to pay tuition fees and thought that they would have to board (live) at the college. Jules' client believed they would have to take out a student loan. Artificial Intelligence responses to questions both clients had asked about going to college!
>
> They are both now aware of where to find accurate information about Further Education and how it differs from Higher Education.

Maintaining an accurate picture of the context in which we practise is crucial. We can gain some of this from reading and exploring online, using multiple sources of information to check for authenticity but also through visits, conferences and conversations.

It is through these that the nuggets of information we can't find online are discovered.

Chris, Jules and their teams undertake regular visits as part of their ongoing CPD. From tattoo parlours to local engineering firms and hotels, these visits have enabled us to broaden our practice and understanding, exploring the choices and pathways open to our clients.

Visits to education and training providers, to discover what courses are like in practice, are vital – not only for growing understanding but also for developing networks and relationships, through which clients can be supported.

It is worth mentioning that we all learn differently; for those among us who struggle to digest and retain pages of written information, visiting, seeing, hearing and experiencing bring the worlds of work and education alive (just as it does for our clients when they go on work experience or open day visits).

> As a CPD challenge, consider for a moment what area of 'careers' scares you? What would you like a client to not ask you? Once you have this, research it. Undertake an occupational report or education study. Use it to focus down and broaden your understanding.
>
> It might be that you need to revisit that which you haven't explored for a while. If you are experienced but have a new client group you are working with, perhaps you need to explore career pathways from the perspective of this client group to check your understanding.

When we first start a new job role, we have no frame of reference.

Things we both did include:

- Researching the most common careers and occupations we were being asked questions about.
- Making route maps for each, so we could understand what was possible for clients. This increases our confidence and provides a foundation and context to practise from.
- Spending time prior to commencing delivery familiarising ourselves with local provision.
- Sharing what we found out with colleagues – and asking them to share with us.

Through reflective practice, having an awareness of where we have gaps in our knowledge helps us to focus our CPD around occupational and educational knowledge. We don't need to be a walking search engine . . . what we do need, though, is an awareness of context, possibilities, and to know where to find the information we need to support our clients via sources which are accurate and valid.

And nobody is great at anything from the outset.

We call what we do 'careers practice' . . . it is called 'practice' for a very good reason! No matter how experienced we become as practitioners, we will always be practising and seeking to be and do better.

It is not a matter of being better than our colleagues but rather better than ourselves yesterday, with an awareness that we will have good days and not so good days; therefore, we should remain kind to ourselves as we grow and develop.

Our definition of what 'better' looks like may change.

Some paradigms that we used ten years ago we no longer use, and/or find we have left behind, as our practice has evolved.

What we do can be seen as an organic thing which has its own beating heart. A bit like the old Tamagotchi toys . . . if we fail to feed it, our practice dies.

You get out of careers practice what you put in.

In most cases, no one is watching; it is us and our client in the room. We can do an adequate job of being a 'careers adviser', and no one will know if we aren't really trying except ourselves.

We will know and, like an unwatered vine, our practice will wither and become bitter.

Yet, if we work at it, try new ways of asking questions or even framing propositions, it will grow and bloom.

We (and your clients) will enjoy the fruits of our endeavours.

 Insider tip

Lifelong learning relates to us as much as our clients. Make time to learn.

Curiosity

People's brains work in all sorts of different ways.

For example, you'll find that some people will welcome an action plan with specific targets and measurable outcomes. This can help some people to take action and to measure their own progress. It can give a sense of moving forward, of success when you achieve, and of making changes in your life. But for some, it may have the opposite effect.

Consider what we do to become physically fit. Why do some people go to a gym while others run solo or lift weights at home? There are pros and cons to both. Running alone can be peaceful, meditative, extremely cost effective and allow a great deal of flexibility. But where is the motivation to do it?

If you're the kind of person who is internally motivated, perhaps you're someone who really enjoys the journey more than the outcome, solo running might be ideal. You enjoy the motion of running. You love the view you get at the top of a hill. You like the feeling at the end of your run when you're tired and perhaps a little sore but your body feels utilised. You feel fitter.

However, if what you anticipate before a run is simply hardship, loneliness and pain, motivation doesn't come easily. Going to the gym means meeting other people, having a trainer to help you set and meet your goals, people congratulate you when you achieve a personal best. It's indoors – so no inclement weather, no dog poo and no massive hills – and because you're paying money for it you want to make the most of the money you spent. Bonus – you get fit! External motivators.

- We're all different.
- We don't all become motivated by the same things or in the same way.
- Be curious.
- Ask your clients what motivates them.

Use these things to help formulate a method of career planning which will actually work for your client.

Some things you might want to ask them:

- What usually makes you want to do something?
- If I send you information, do you think you'll read it – honestly!?
- How do you like to find out about things?
- How do you make choices? Give me an example.
- Do you find it easier if you have someone else to do things with?

So, when a client comes back to you having completed none of the actions on their action plan, rather than attributing 'blame' for their inaction . . . or being defensive ('I did tell them what they should do') . . . ask *'why?'*

- Why didn't this form of planning suit them?
- What would work for them?
- What are the things that engage them in their life and choices?

And, likewise, we all operate differently as careers practitioners. Indulge your own curiosity by finding out how others work. Observe your colleagues, ask questions, try out something you've seen which you wouldn't normally do, even if you don't have time allocated to visit employers. Be curious in your day-to-day life. When your car is getting a windscreen replaced, your boiler is being fixed or you are waiting to collect a friend from hospital . . . ask questions . . . sit and watch . . . find out how and why the members of staff do what they do.

Exploring CPD outside the echo chamber of the careers sphere is important to widen our sense of what is possible and stretch our careers practice. It also helps us understand that there is life and different perceptions/ways of looking at the world beyond our own community.

Chris has recently been following Vinh Giang for his insights into public speaking and Simon Sinek as part of his CPD as a manager. Both have helped him to consider how to connect with different people; neither is in the 'careers sphere' but both have been incredibly helpful in developing Chris' skills within his practice.

Such learning is useful, as it keeps us open and questioning. It is worth remembering that not everyone speaks the language of our careers sphere. Some people will not know where we are coming from or what we mean, nor will they be as excited about what we do. Being able to translate our enthusiasm into terms that others can relate to is crucial.

 Insider tip

Careers practitioners are curious cats . . . our greatest strength is a desire to understand how the world works and how people think and relate to the world. Such curiosity feeds our questions and how we help and support our clients. Stay curious!

D

Decisions

There has often been pressure within career guidance on helping clients to make decisions in a single careers session, often weighing up choice A and choice B, using just pros and cons.

Decision-making is often far more subtle than this.

For a few clients, the above, somewhat one-dimensional approach might work.

Most of us, however, need time to process ideas and reflect.

Our role can help clients to consider a wider viewpoint on decision-making – helping them to consider how they wish to decide, how much time they need and what they need to do to help them make a decision; it is no longer exclusively about helping them make a choice in a single session!

Some will require several sessions to work through their ideas. Some may need to see us and then go and do some research or undertake some experiential learning before returning for further support. Others will find their careers guidance session a catalyst for change, which kicks off a greater exploration of their hopes and dreams.

Even on occasions where clients have seemingly made a decision to do X or Y in the future, when we catch up with them weeks or months later, their ideas are often totally different. The guidance session started them thinking far more deeply about what they wanted to do, becoming a 'kick start' to think more deeply.

> One student planned their next steps to find an apprenticeship. They considered carefully the steps to help with their transition.
>
> The student came back about a month later and said they were now on another path. As we unpicked things, they said the reality of actually planning to do an apprenticeship helped them realise that it wasn't what they really wanted to do; it was a fantasy.
>
> This idea of a 'fantasy stage' aligns with Ginzberg's developmental theory; the guidance process made the career real to the student and then on reflection, helped them to realise that their initial choice (and plan of action) was the wrong one for them at this time.

When a decision is made in a session, it is often beneficial for clients to consider how much time they may need to reflect on their choice, to ensure it is the right one for them.

Mental health significantly impacts decision-making processes.

Conditions like schizophrenia, depression and anxiety can affect how individuals evaluate risks and rewards, leading to impaired judgement and potentially poor choices.

The ability to make decisions can also be influenced by other factors like stress, illness and simply poor judgement.

- Executive function: Mental health conditions can affect executive function, which includes skills like planning, organising and making choices.
- Cognitive impairments: Some mental health conditions can cause cognitive impairments, such as impaired attention, working memory or response inhibition, which can lead to flawed decision-making.
- Emotional influences: Emotions play a crucial role in decision-making. Positive emotions can lead to risk-taking, while negative emotions can make individuals more risk-averse.

Anxiety

When our brain senses anxiety, it prepares for survival mode and enters what is called a positive stress state, where an increase in blood flow and oxygen to the brain leads to greater cognitive performance.

However, when anxiety is not managed, the body shifts to a negative stress, or toxic stress, state which has the opposite effect. There is a decrease in blood flow and oxygen to the brain, which promotes lower cognitive functioning and sends the brain into a chaotic state. In this state, the brain is unable to access the information it needs to make logical decisions.

Stress

One way that stress can affect decision-making is by limiting the ability to make novel decisions and adapt to change. For example, a 2012 study found that participants who were subjected to the stress of preparing for a medical selection exam tended to make decisions out of habit, whereas participants who were not under the same stress were able to make new decisions, adapting them to the situation at hand and the perceived consequences. Researchers concluded that 'the brain resorts to habitual decision making because it exerts less demands on our cognitive resources'.[1]

The more decisions we make in a day, the more stressed out we become. The phenomenon of decision-making fatigue states that the more decisions we make in a day, the harder it will be to make additional clear-headed decisions. Also referred to as ego depletion, it's as if the brain has only a limited capacity to make decisions, and once this capacity is depleted, there's little left.

It is crucial to be mindful of our own state when supporting others as we may also struggle if we are in a similar state. It is crucial for us to remember that decisions can't be forced through.

Returning to our Rogerian core conditions[2] (empathy, congruence and unconditional positive regard) is a useful reminder of what we are doing and why.

> Other theories which link to career planning include Donald Super's developmental theory,[3] which considers the importance of exploration as part of growing our 'opportunity awareness' and 'decision-making'; as well as other key elements relating to how we maintain and develop our careers.

---

1 https://thedecisionlab.com/insights/health/stress-redesigns-decision-making/
2 https://counsellingtutor.com/counselling-approaches/person-centred-approach-to-counselling/carl-rogers-core-conditions
3 https://www.careers.govt.nz/resources/career-practice/career-theory-models/supers-theory/

There is an argument to be had that the timelines which Ginzberg and Super align with their fantasy and explorative phases coincide with the latest understanding regarding the teenage brain and the prefrontal cortex[4] and how this affects decision-making.[5]

Some of the latest research regarding neurodivergence indicates a delay in the development of the prefrontal cortex[6] – from this we could argue neurodivergent young people may remain for longer in the 'fantasy' and 'explorative' phases.

Reading beyond the careers sphere is vital to ensure that we remain informed about brain development and career thinking.

There is debate around the effects nature, nurture and culture may have on what we consider the developmental stages. Aspects of Bill Law's community interaction theory touch upon this.[7] This theory is worth being aware of in our work supporting clients with learning support needs as there is a risk we will collude with social norms and, in doing so, be complicit in closing down opportunities for our clients.

Other commentators, such as Gideon Arulmani, also considers the very idea of a 'career' as a cultural construct.[8] As such, we must be wary of applying predominantly Western definitions of what a career is or isn't and whether the life stages we discuss in career theories are inherent to everyone or represent a social construct largely found within late 20th- and early 21st-century Western cultures.

We should be mindful that there are other models of career planning and management which, as practitioners, should form part of our continual professional development as we seek out alternative perspectives.

 Insider tip

Try asking 'What do you mean by that?' or 'Explain how you think about that?'

---

4 https://careerswriters.com/2024/04/17/risk-and-decision-making
5 https://www.choosingtherapy.com/adhd-brain-vs-normal-brain
6 https://www.thelancet.com/journals/lanpsy/article/PIIS2215-0366(17)30049-4/abstract and https://www.nature.com/articles/s41598-020-59921-4
7 https://marcr.net/marcr-for-career-professionals/career-theory/career-theories-and-theorists/community-interaction-theory
8 http://thepromisefoundation.org/career-and-livelihood-planning

Good reads

- *Creative Coaching: Theory into Practice* by Hambly and Bomford considers strategies to support decision-making.
- And coming out next year – *The Career Development Professional's Handbook of Mental Health: Practical Strategies for Promoting Wellbeing*, Liane Hambly and Dr Oliver Jenkin.

Designing your day

Let's have a look in a bit more depth at some of the ways you can structure a day. You'll need to get to your setting first (see the chapter on *Going Places*).

Being mindful of our personal headspace and whether we are thirsty or hungry is really important. Schedule in breaks and ensure you take your lunch . . . it's amazing how easy it is to forget to look after ourselves and, in doing so, not be in the headspace to support our clients.

This also applies to our clients. It's worth being mindful that some clients come from complex backgrounds where food or space may be scarce.

Some settings provide breakfast for their students, as they understand the link between hunger and an inability to learn in a school setting. This explicit understanding is great to see.

Questions to ask yourself and discuss with your setting:

- When will sessions start?
- How long is each session?
- How many sessions are being delivered across the day?
- Will you run a lunchtime drop-in session?
- Is there time to talk through cases at the end of the day?
- Is there access to Wi-Fi?
- What is the room setup?

These questions deal with the detail of what you will be doing and may be affected by the organisation you work for and their policies. We would encourage you to advocate for what is ultimately best for your clients.

We say this with the awareness that within organisational and financial pressures, this might not always be easy!

As a profession, CDPs are client-centred and follow a specific Code of Ethics which sets us apart from those who are unqualified or are within different professions working in similar arenas. Our ethics also provide us with a specific rationale for what we do, how we do it and why.

Career Development Institute (CDI) ethics are not based on whimsy or fluffy 'niceness'; they are based on research and the experiences of previous generations on whose shoulders we stand. They are central to who we are and what we do, forming a pivot to the discussions in regard to how we work. You can find a link to the CDI Code of Ethics in the *Zone* at the end of this book.

- Learn how to keep to time. It's an art (takes practice) to bring each session to its end on time and then to clear our heads ready for the next one.
- Avoid thinking about the last session while starting the next.
- Avoid thinking about the socks in the washing machine (e.g. the chores which need doing at home or in the office); be in the moment with each client. Be present.
- Take breaks.

> Have a look at the CDI paper on the role of a careers adviser. Link is in the *Zone*.

Length of session

Many of us will be aware that the recommendations for individual career sessions is 'at least 45 minutes', with a strong evidence base indicating this is the ideal minimum length of time for a careers session to allow time for both exploration and self-discovery.

This does not mean every appointment should last 45 minutes!

Being client-centred takes priority – considering what our clients need must come first.

For example, for some clients 45 minutes is too long for them to sit still in a session (they would be metaphorically climbing the walls!). To build in the flexibility for clients with learning support needs is important for successful careers sessions. So how can this be done?

There are several possibilities:

Fixed but flexible

Sessions are fixed, with up to one hour per session (depending on the clients' needs).

Have an agreement with the school to shorten the sessions if needed and to have the option to 'walk and talk' with clients. For many clients who struggle in the formal setting of a room, with a traditional desk and table setup, this can be useful to enable engagement.

Clients who need to move can have their careers session while we walk around a communal area or outside space together. Agree which space(s) you can use without disturbing others and establish a system to safeguard yourself and your clients.

> How to be safe in a space:
> - Make sure someone knows you are going there, how long you are likely to be and who you are with.
> - Stay visible to other staff – as long as someone can see you from a window you aren't 'missing'.
> - Check before you start your day that none of the clients you will be seeing have any circumstances or needs which would make walking with them, or sitting on a swing seat outside, risky for either of you.

Drop-ins

Drop-ins are another solution and can take lots of different forms and be run in a wide range of different settings, but appropriate consideration does need to be given to your own wellbeing to ensure you get a break!

Drop-in sessions (often at lunch and/or break time) during a fixed window of time allow students to access careers guidance on their terms, outside the formal parameters of booked appointments.

They can be incredibly empowering if handled with the care of a standard (booked) careers session.

This is an example of how drop-ins can have an impact:

> A client looking at Post-16 options was too anxious to come to their booked 'official careers appointment':
>
> Several attempts had been made to see them, including seeing if they would attend with support from their teaching assistant or favourite tutor. They still couldn't cope with attending.
>
> Offered and advertised, to students (on the school website, on school social media platforms, and the school newsletter which went to students, teachers, parents, and carers) was a lunchtime drop-in.

> The drop-in was for twenty minutes at the start of the lunch period, with the rest of the time over lunch available for lunch.
>
> Our student rocked up one day out of 'curiosity' to see what it was like; they asked questions – what do you do? Why? – and left after ten minutes.
>
> The next week they rocked up again; they said that they had 'no idea what they were going to do after Year 11' . . . before leaving ten minutes later, after a gentle initial chat about their worries.
>
> The following week. Who should turn up, but our student! . . .
>
> saying 'There is no way I am going to college! You can't make me apply or do anything!' which was discussed with clear messaging that we never tell people what to do! We discuss ideas and listen to them. Again, off they went after fifteen minutes.
>
> The following week, they popped by again with a smile.
>
> . . . and so it continued for about a term and a half. They would pop by each week and continue to explore their ideas and talk about their thoughts since the previous week (ten to fifteen minutes at a time). By the end of this, they had applied to college for a course they loved the idea of.
>
> A bit of prep followed: some gentle interview practice in the drop-in (how to shake hands and looking just above and between the eyes if struggling to make eye contact).
>
> At the end of term they popped by with a huge grin on their face . . . 'I'm going to college, I was accepted after interview' ☺ #careersimpact
>
> Offering drop-ins helped to create an inclusive service which was client-centred.

They don't need to be at lunchtime . . . or just for students.

You can consider:

- Before/after school sessions;
- Careers week drop-in;
- Coffee mornings.
  These can also be attended by parents, teachers or carers wanting to find out more about how to support their young adults.

Thirty-minute fixed session (with repeats available)

Thirty-minute sessions, where students will have more than one session based on their needs.

The initial 30-minute session is to see where they are at and how things are going, as well as to help the client understand what is possible within the remit of a careers guidance session and how the client and adviser will work together.

It can also be used to build a focus for following sessions.

Repeat session(s) – depending on need – are then used to provide interventions focused on their needs.

For some clients, the 30-minute session can be enough to resolve their concerns, but from experience, this is a rarity.

A good example of where this format has worked well:

A student who was unsure what they wanted to try out; they were anxious and had been putting themselves under pressure. Signs of stress were 'pinging' off them.

- We had agreed in advance to work together for just 30 minutes, to reduce their anxiety.
- To help them identify what they wanted to explore, we agreed to try a card sort (using job cards with names of different occupations on). In this instance, the Panjango Trump cards.
- We agreed that we wouldn't make any decisions nor judgement about what 'came up' from this; we would just identify possibilities (to revisit in our next 30-minute session).
- The client sorted their cards into three piles, representing what they 'definitely didn't like', 'what interested them' and 'maybes' represented by ☹ ☺ ❓
- Once they had done this, they sorted the ☺ pile into patterns (importantly based on *their* ideas/values and concepts).
- Next they considered whether any of the ❓ (maybe) cards should be added.

From this came a discussion as to what was meaningful for them as patterns of possibility. We summarised and left the session with an agreement to revisit these possibilities in our next session.

This gave them the space to stop and think without pressure, resulting in a productive session.

What did we cover in repeat sessions?

- Revisit the photographs of the card sort.
- Explore what we would do next.
- Agree to identify the top three 'options/jobs' which interested them and that they would then like to 'try out'.
- Find three which appealed to them – hairdressing, retail, comic book illustration.
- Discuss how they would like to explore these areas and 'try them out'.

Some of the previous work we had done in the 'career introductions' had explored that many of us won't know what we wish to do until we are closer to 25.

The student decided they wished to work with the work experience coordinator in the college to find supported work experience in hairdressing and search for a part-time job in retail.

In addition, they would work with the art teacher in the college to explore making their own comics.

This provided them with a way forward which wouldn't have been possible without taking the pressure off by splitting the session into two halves.

#careersimpact

If you want to find out more about developmental career theory, follow the link in our *Zone* titled *When Do We Know?*

Flexed appointments

A flexible model, where the length of the session is dictated by the needs of the clients.

This is agreed in advance with the setting and works really well in specialist settings with small class sizes and a wide variety of needs among the students.

Start the year by going in and delivering a gentle introduction to the different groups of students. Make sure the staff get involved so that they also know what will be happening for their students.

Discuss with them what the careers sessions are like, including confidentiality (with exceptions for health and safety and sharing of action plans with their tutor and parents/carers with their permission), as well as an explanation of how the sessions are client-led.

Agree how the students will be prioritised and invited to appointments. Ask about when is good for them.

Crucially, clients remain in control of the length of time of each session, the format of action plans and to a certain extent the location of the session.

- For clients with high levels of anxiety, this sense of control can be incredibly useful in enabling sessions to be productive. As well as clients being told in advance (if booked in) which includes when they will be 'seen' (morning or afternoon) and by whom.

Flow

Jules' preferred structure, particularly in specialist settings, is to have a running order of students with approximate timings. Each student knows who they come before and after. Not only does this avoid students having to wait outside a room for the previous student to finish, it also gives time for regulation before and after interventions. Body movement and spaces of silence while engaged in a joint activity help to regulate emotions and thinking.

While walking together, Jules will use rhetorical questions as a means of engagement without the need for chit-chat (which can drain energy for many neurodivergent people).

Using rhetorical questions:

- Use chatty comments that need no answer – typically these could start with 'I wonder . . .' or could be statements such as 'what an interesting picture' or non-directed questions like 'how on earth do you make a cake out of those ingredients?'
- Leave open-ended and personal questions until later.
- Comments outweigh questions!

In some settings, where students are able to get themselves safely to and from appointments but are likely to be anxious about talking to an unfamiliar person, Jules asks each student to fetch the next and to tell them what Jules does. This helps students to reflect on what they gained from their guidance and allays anxiety for new clients. Some of the explanations have been super helpful . . . 'It's ok to just be yourself', 'she's useful – she has a huge brain', 'there aren't any wrong answers', 'it doesn't matter if you know what you want to do or not'.

After a session, there is nothing wrong with saying that you need to delay your next session by a couple of minutes (or even five minutes) so you can have a breather and get your head together. This is especially important if we have just dealt with a particularly tricky situation (such as a child protection issue), or it could have been a session which was clunky or just mentally draining.

> As part of day-to-day arrangements (precautions), if there are issues which need to be dealt with before starting the next session (such as child protection or safeguarding), having procedures in place with our settings to deal with these, such as being able to cancel the next appointment(s) and rebook them for a later time if required, is important – to give us time to complete paperwork and meet with those we need to (keeping clients safe).

Take the time you need to sit and catch your thoughts, or even take yourself outside to literally get some fresh air.

You are no good to your next client if your mind is still reeling due to the previous session.

Regulate  Relate  Reason

Accurate recording

What you record, and how you record it, matters. Use words that are factual, not emotive or containing opinion. Make sure dates and data are accurate at the time of recording. And ensure you record all your interventions within a few days of delivery. If your current schedule doesn't allow this . . . change your schedule!

Why?

- It ensures any ongoing support of your client will build on what you have already done.
- The law, and probably your contract, will require it.
- It promotes continuity of support and communication with other agencies when they are involved.
- It helps identify patterns and challenges in a person's life. This is particularly important in identifying safeguarding issues, but will also help you to recognise patterns of decision-making and career planning.
- It is key to accountability – to people who use services, to managers, to inspections and audits.
- It is evidence – for court, complaints and investigations.

Insider tips

Embrace that flow state when you are providing guidance; in this place, peace can be found.

Developing an internal clock that will help you finish each individual career session on time and not overrun!

Make sure you leave time for your admin.

Difficult conversations

Difficult conversations are a part of life as a CDP.

We walk the line between clients, their families and those who run the provisions we work in, whether schools, colleges or community settings. Sometimes we won't be able to please all the people all of the time, which can make it hard to manage or navigate the myriad multiple agendas in play.

These are examples of some of the difficult conversations we've been faced with over the years and what we did to manage them:

Careers work doesn't really matter or isn't important
This can be the hardest of challenges to face when you go into an establishment and they are clearly just ticking a box. You aren't valued, and at worst seen as a nuisance or a threat to what they see their agenda as.

There can be an indifference to the work we are doing, and it can be very difficult to engage these settings with the follow-up support that can be the make or break for some of our clients.

One solution is reframing the situation for ourselves and putting the clients at the centre of the picture we are seeing (changing the perspective).

- We are there to serve and help our clients. If we weren't there, they might have no one to talk to whom they trust, nor access to understanding all of their options.

In some settings, this can be a real motivator, especially when you receive feedback that supports this from the students or their parents/carers.

An alternative is working slowly with the setting to build trust and provide evidence from impact studies and feedback, to show why the careers work does matter.

- Key to this is providing evidence that meets the KPIs (Key Performance Indicators) of those who you are seeking to influence (often those in positions of power); showing how you can solve one or more of their problems. Whether this is evidence of how independent careers guidance reduces the number of those with no fixed onward destination or improves the mental health and wellbeing of the clients we have seen.
  - Speaking their language – sometimes you will find yourself in the situation where you are advocating for the careers service you are aiming to deliver and, no matter how much you describe the social good or positive effects on wellbeing the service will have, the member

of leadership you are talking to just doesn't get it or isn't invested, creating barriers to delivery and the success of the given project or delivery you are trying to offer. A shift in language – not literally speaking another language but one which speaks to their world view or KPIs (to what they are measured on) can work wonders. For example, if they are targeted to reduce the number of clients falling NEET (Not in Education Employment or Training) then focusing on evidence of how your delivery will help them meet this target can work wonders.

- It may take several years for this impact data to be available, so be prepared to have patience.
- When setting up delivery with partners, communicate clearly about expectations such as action plan formats, session length and paperwork from the start, so everyone is on the same page. Often, dissatisfaction arises from miscommunication around expectations. Tackling this from the start heads this off at the pass.

You must do shorter career sessions

A huge pressure in many settings in England is a lack of time, resources and therefore a desire for some institutions to run shorter career sessions, based on the idea that the Careers Professional will then be able to see more students and have a wider impact.

- This builds on the metric that the quantity of clients seen is the best way to measure success. Gatsby Benchmark 8 in England is unhelpful in this respect as it only requires a measure of who has received 1:1 personal guidance as a one-off.

The recommendation of at least 45 minutes per session, and more sessions for learners who are vulnerable, is based on experience of impact.

We know as professionals that by providing longer sessions to fewer students, our impact is greater; less is more.

Yet how can we persuade our settings and, in some instances, those who set the contract requirements?

It will of course vary considerably on the setting you find yourself in and the extent to which you have leeway to challenge; this will change depending upon context.

Different ways to handle the situation, to push for longer sessions or reach a compromise include:

- Run a controlled trial by offering some students ten-minute sessions and others longer sessions – evaluate the impact and outcomes. Use evidence-based practice to show the effectiveness of longer sessions.

- Find a middle ground, where the whole of the cohort isn't seen and you combine shorter appointments to identify needs or group guidance sessions to support and identify needs, with longer appointments for targeted clients; this is a triage-based approach.
- Hold out for best practice and refuse to deliver shorter sessions, quoting the evidence and CDI Code of Ethics, is a position that can be taken. It's bold and something which can be considered. It comes with a warning ... There is a very real risk that your job could be placed at risk if doing so, depending on who you are working for. So, talk to your managers. Offer solutions. Be united in your approach.
- To explore more about group guidance, a good starting point is the Textures of Groupwork model, as published by Sue Edwards, senior lecturer in career guidance at the University of Huddersfield, and by joining the LinkedIn Group Guidance for career practitioners.

 Good read

Forthcoming title: *Group Career Guidance and Coaching* by Sue Edwards, Susan Meldrum, Emma Anderson and Emma Hill. Keep a lookout for it on the Trotman website.

You need to fill up our sixth form or local college

An insidious situation to find ourselves in is when we are placed under pressure to direct clients to a specified outcome, such as being asked to 'fill up or promote' a sixth form, or not make students aware of specialist provision (which usually costs more).

This is when there is an overarching agenda of a presiding institution or group.

Navigating this can be difficult, especially if you are directly employed by an institution that also controls your pay packet and also has a hold over you regarding the direction of your career.

- In the first instance, referring to the CDI or AGCAS Code of Ethics which stipulates our duty to remain independent and provide guidance on all pathways is the lynchpin of what we do.

In a recent interview for a job with an independent provider, Jules raised this issue with the CEO. The job spec had cited a requirement to promote the provider. Jules asked why this was necessary. Surely if the provision is suitable and good, there is no need for this – as per Jules' Code of Ethics, she would always support clients to look at alternatives. But if the provision was the best fit for them, the client would choose it. The CEO reflected that this was a better professional standpoint and offered to rethink the job spec!

A discussion about best practice and referring to the evidence base for independent careers guidance can be a good starting point – making our case.

However, the financial incentives of the system for sixth forms and colleges to fill the places on their courses, as well as the necessity of bills to pay, can be an overriding factor in some settings.

- Changing the discussion away from the client-centred duty to attend to their institutional drivers can be useful (make your provision the best and people will want to come here!).
- If a student understands why their given choice can benefit them, they are more likely to stay or choose that path. This can be a result of independent guidance.

We may be placed under pressure to not provide details of the other choices (that aren't at that institution). When it comes to this, it can be a test of conviction and our individual moral or ethical compass. It is also a test of the priorities of that organisation and the extent to which they will bend or break with their values, or whether they align their values with prioritising the number of students they take on and creating income; rather than being client-centred.

Being client-centred and focusing on the economic needs of an institution are not mutually exclusive.

At one school where Chris works, the headteacher stands up to talk to the Year 11 students and their parents/carers at his school sixth form open evening. At this evening, each year he will say, 'The sixth form isn't for everyone and students should ensure that, if they decide to come to sixth form, it meets their needs. If they are unsure or want to know what other options they have, they should speak to our independent career adviser.'

As a leader, he has the courage of his convictions and is ethical to his core, placing the needs of the students first.

His sixth form is successful and none of the Year 11 students face 'pressure' to attend the sixth form – it is their choice.

There's no point in 'inclusive approaches'
Liane Hambly, author of *Creative Career Coaching – Theory into Practice*, asked recently . . . how do you get senior leadership in schools to buy into inclusive approaches?

Ideas:

- Run a small trial . . . just one day to do it our way and then assess the impact.
- Switch the language so you show how an inclusive approach will meet their management needs.
- Appeal to their egos and explain how amazing they will look in the eyes of their governors and parents/carers.
- If they are genuinely client-centred, explore how the impact is greater and results are more positive for the mental health of clients.

You can't have a room

A common conversation which we've had in lots of different settings is the one where we are told 'You can't have a room' or 'There isn't any space' or 'You're not a teacher, so you have to work in the canteen' or 'It just isn't possible.'

Often this is presented as an intractable issue by the setting we are in.

- A gentle approach is often a good starting point, explaining how careers work is confidential and why it needs a private setting.
- Ask them to consider how they would feel if it was their child who was sharing their hopes and dreams in an open space, where others were walking by has worked in the past to help settings reevaluate their position.
- Make it part of the delivery arrangements from the start, if you have the means to do so. Agreeing a suitable venue and room at the start of agreeing a service is useful.
- Have a discussion about how clients could be affected and be reluctant to open up if they are aware others are present or there is the possibility of teachers overhearing. There is the hidden pressure of knowing teachers are present, as students may be reluctant to talk openly in such situations.

Decide how bold you are prepared to be!

Clients who say 'I dunno' or 'I don't know'

For many younger students in schools, and those with a developmental delay or block in their career thinking, it is quite normal for them to not know what they want to do.

Even for older clients who have faced disruption or found themselves stuck, not knowing is also part of their career landscape.

In many cases, the initial 'I don't know' response hides a wealth of anxiety and uncertainty. Saying 'I don't know' remains a way to keep themselves safe. It is a good deflection and form of self-defence.

In many settings, you can see this learnt behaviour with some students who keep staff at bay by this common reply. In doing so, teachers might not ask questions of them again and let things go. As a strategy, it can be really effective.

Strategies we can use include:

Change the question
Instead of asking 'What do you want to do or be when you are older?' ask 'How far have you got with thinking about the future?' This provides a much broader platform or launch pad to have a conversation from. It doesn't assume that a career discussion is X, Y or Z and allows for a more holistic approach.

Slow down – or stop!
Trying to rush clients who are stuck for a decision is counterproductive. Placing unwarranted pressure doesn't aid decision-making. When many of us think about the big decisions we are making, we need to take time to reflect and think. Very rarely do we make a pros and cons list and make a decision then and there.

A client became visibly anxious in a careers session with Jules after being asked whether they had any ideas for the future. Jules stopped – telling the client she had noticed their anxiety. She suggested a different activity for a while – playing with a variety of sensory toys to see what worked well for Jules and for the young person. After re-assuring the young person that it was fine to do this activity as part of a careers session – because it helps your brain work again – it transpired that they found the softer items (a feather, a piece of velvet and pipe cleaners) helped them regulate. The conversation restarted naturally, and the young person was able to explain that they were being asked all the time by people to say what they wanted for the future. They knew they needed to think about it but every time they were asked it felt like their 'brain would explode'. The agreed action following this was for staff to be informed (by both Jules and the young person), and that they could take the soft sensory items with them. This young person came to find Jules at lunchtime – said they'd been crying 'in a good way' and had told their tutor how they felt. Within a few weeks they chose to do a higher level qualification which they have now successfully completed.

Find out what 'I don't know' means
If you notice this is a patterned response, give your client some options . . . 'I've noticed you have answered with "I don't know" a few times. It would really help me to know what this means – that way I can make some suggestions that suit you and the way your brain works. Does it mean "I don't understand the question", "I can't put my answer into the right words", "I don't want to talk right now", "I need more time to think", "I don't think you will like my answer"?'

Jules worked with a client recently who was referred by their education provider – they had been trying to find the young person a suitable work option to move on to. They had tried numerous work placements and visited different employers but kept getting an 'I don't know' response. After chatting about what 'I don't know' meant, it transpired that the thought of working was so anxiety provoking for this young person that it made them 'want to gnaw my own arm off'! They just did not want to tell staff because they were aware that staff were only trying to 'help and do their job'.

Meaningful results and outcomes come from recognising and applying the models and theories we have learnt.

From looking at our own practices and that of others, we've observed that it seems to be approaches which are focused just on pushing the agenda of positive outcomes such as education or not falling NEET (Not in Education, Employment or Training etc.) which often fail in the long term, as they fail to take into account the client as a whole.

Positive outcomes are often the results of high-quality client-centred careers guidance, rather than interactions which are led by the agenda of 'EET outcomes' as their focus or sole aim.

Let go
Some clients don't follow through with their action plans or change their minds about their next steps. This can cause us to ask, 'Have I failed them?' 'Was I a rubbish Careers Adviser?' as they hadn't done what we had talked about.

For many clients, the process of career guidance, of discussing possibilities, is in itself a catalyst to the meaningful outcome they were seeking. Once you 'let go' in your practice and stop trying so hard to encourage or cajole clients into Education, Employment or Training (EET), the results from guidance sessions become so much better.

Appreciate that pathways which aren't within immediate EET outcomes are just as valid; from going travelling to taking a mental health break.

When we stop trying to push and find flow, our careers work becomes so much more impactful.

 Authors' note

Chris had a student recently who changed their mind following the session which explored how to be a chef. They had gone through the options and how to get there, how they were going to research college courses and apply.

A week later, Chris received an email from a teacher saying that the young person had changed their mind and was now looking at a different career area.

Chris caught up with them the following week in passing and discussed what had happened (primarily to check if they were okay, and secondly as an opportunity to get feedback, which helps us to grow and develop as practitioners).

They said the session had been really helpful as it really got them thinking – which they hadn't done before.

Going through the motions of discussing what they would actually need to do to become a chef and applying for college or searching for apprenticeships made them realise this wasn't for them. They thanked Chris for the session.

This helped Chris to understand how he had been of service to them.

 Insider tip

Whatever you do, don't bite when clients (or other professionals) try and get you to react or get a rise out of you.

Disabled

If you have a long-term and/or hidden health condition, illness or disability it can be challenging to manage ongoing work alongside health issues. Seeking out disability-confident employers can be a useful way of ensuring that you have a much greater chance of accessing the support you need, as well as being aware of the rules around sharing your condition and the support you have a right to access. You have a right to reasonable adjustments. Employers and service providers must make changes to policies, practices or physical environments to accommodate disabled people. If you need help to specify the adjustments that might suit you best, there are numerous organisations who can help. The Disability Rights UK website – link in the *Zone* – is an excellent place to start.

Inclusive work practices and flexible working, including contractual arrangements and hybrid working, can make a massive difference to those affected by short- and long-term conditions. Talking to your employer (if possible) about what reasonable adjustments and considerations you need to thrive can make a big difference. However, we are aware that not all employers are accommodating or supportive, so understanding your rights and being informed is important, as well as being mindful of your individual situation.

Many of us have family and friends with life-limiting conditions and are acutely aware that each person's responses and ways of coping are different. Some are battling significant mental health issues and others appear to be striving, with humour.

How our private and public personas, as well as our inner lives, cope with such circumstances can be wildly different. Sometimes, putting on a brave face may be part of our strategy for survival, rather than denial (which others may assume); it might also be part of an implicit, or even explicit, strategy in dealing with ableism within wider society. Especially when some areas of society struggle with engaging positively with any form of disability or illness (hidden or visible).

Being aware in our careers work, wherever we find ourselves working, that not all clients will be in a good place to explore career ideas, or even want to, is something that as career practitioners we need to be sensitive to. Physical illness and mental ill health are important factors to be considered.

Careers coach and writer Polly Wiggins makes some important points with regard to this and careers work:

> 'Career people can be a bit careers-obsessed (which is true of most motivated professionals!) and forget that not everyone sees career in the way we do – for some, it's just not that important. For others, they might want to prioritise their career, but the reality of their current context might supersede that (whether that's for health reasons, financial reasons etc.) ... also (it's) worth pointing out that society is much, much happier about people with disabilities who are positive and upbeat about disability ... How people present their illness/disabilities might have far more to do with managing the reactions of others than it is about representing their true feelings. I certainly know I am very careful about how I talk about my own illness, in an attempt (mostly successful) to avoid stigma.'

Talking about pain, Polly goes on to say *'it does tend to be valorised by society (one of the reasons we look up to sports stars so much), but chronic pain is rarely glamorous, inspiring or motivational. Suffering does not always lead to growth; sometimes it's just miserable. . . . I think careers coaching can be a really useful chance for people to reflect on and unpick their work-based philosophies, to make sure their beliefs are still serving them.'*

 Good read

- For those of you interested in Disability, Impairments and Inclusion, do have a read of our first book: *Career Development and Inclusive Practice*.

Disclosure and barring

The Disclosure and Barring Service (DBS) helps employers make safer recruitment decisions each year by processing and issuing DBS checks for England, Wales, the Channel Islands and the Isle of Man. DBS also maintains the Adults' and Children's Barred Lists, and makes considered decisions as to whether an individual should be included on one or both of these lists and barred from engaging in regulated activity.

In Northern Ireland, the checks are issued by AccessNI, using the DBS.

In Scotland, Disclosure Scotland checks are similar to DBS checks but are only available for people working in Scotland.

Disclosure teams carry out DBS checks (previously known as CRB, or criminal record checks).

There are four types of DBS check, and each type results in a DBS certificate being issued to an individual. Employers can then ask to see the certificate to ensure that they are recruiting suitable people.

The four levels of DBS check are:

- Basic DBS check;
- Standard DBS check;
- Enhanced DBS check; and
- Enhanced with Barred List(s) DBS check.

The information contained on each type of check is different.

- You may be asked to show a physical copy of your certificate to a setting before being allowed to work there.
- If you are working in a role where you will frequently come into contact with children and adults with care and support needs, it is likely you will need an enhanced check.

A Basic DBS check is for any purpose, including employment. The certificate will contain details of convictions and conditional cautions that are considered to be unspent under the terms of the Rehabilitation of Offenders Act (ROA) 1974.

An individual can apply for a Basic check directly to DBS online, or an employer can apply for a basic check on an individual's behalf, through a Responsible Organisation, if they have consent.

A Standard DBS check is suitable for certain roles, such as a security guard. The certificate will contain details of both spent and unspent convictions, cautions, reprimands and warnings that are held on the Police National Computer, which are not subject to filtering.

An individual cannot apply for a standard check by themselves. There must be a recruiting organisation who needs the applicant to get the check. This is then sent to DBS through a Registered Body.

- The service is free for volunteers.

An Enhanced DBS check is suitable for people working with children or adults in certain circumstances such as those in receipt of healthcare or personal care. An Enhanced DBS check is also suitable for a small number of other roles such as taxi licence applications or people working in the Gambling Commission.

The certificate will contain the same details as a standard certificate and, if the role is eligible, an employer can request that one or both of the DBS Barred Lists are checked.

The certificate may also contain non-conviction information supplied by relevant police forces, if it is deemed relevant and ought to be contained in the certificate.

An individual cannot apply for an Enhanced DBS check by themselves. There must be a recruiting organisation who needs the applicant to get the check. In England, there are numbers of CDPs who are self-employed or sole traders. A self-employed person who is eligible for a Standard or Enhanced DBS check can ask the organisation that wishes to contract their services to apply for their check; they can also ask a local authority or a governing body.

Eligibility
Eligibility for Standard, Enhanced and Enhanced with Barred Lists DBS checks is prescribed in legislation. Recruiters should only request a DBS check on an individual when they are legally allowed to do so – they must be entitled by law to ask an individual to reveal their full criminal history. This is known as asking 'an exempted question'.

We have put links to more information in the *Zone*.

E

Emails

The curse and blessing of emails! Although a modern boon, helping us to set up arrangements and bookings faster than in days of yore, they are also a curse. Creating work and sapping our time and energy, as they are so easy to send and receive.

The number of people we know within the careers sector (and outside of it) who have found their time consumed by trying to keep on top of emails is countless.

These are our top tips for helping to ensure that emails don't clog up your delivery.

1. Use your email settings to block spam.
2. Only check emails if you have the time to deal with them.
3. Pick up the phone . . . sometimes a phone call or arranging to meet face to face is so much more productive than playing email ping pong.
4. Use emails to book meetings (whether face to face or over video calling) to discuss and resolve things. This can reduce the protracted back and forth of emails for both parties.
5. Ask yourself if the email you are sending is purposeful for both you and the recipient.
6. Open emails once and deal with them at that time . . . either delete or reply.
7. Say no. It is so easy to say yes to things via email and not consider whether you actually have the time to deal with whatever you are agreeing to. Don't overcommit via email.

8. Don't try and check emails in between clients; it means you aren't present for your clients and you aren't considering what you are writing in your emails (risking errors).

9. Slow down (this one is really hard for both of us!). Stop and consider how you are replying before sending an email. The desire to 'deal' with emails quickly means we risk making mistakes. We've put some ideas on how to slow down in the *Fast or Slow* section.

10. Don't reply to emails in anger or haste – this leads to emails which will bite you on the bum. You will not word things sensitively or well, might make an ill-thought or badly timed comment, and could upset others or get yourself into trouble. There is no dialogue between two angry people!

11. Consider what you write in emails. Write assuming that someone else to whom you didn't send the email will read it. We imagine that emails are private conversations between two or more parties. In reality, they are conversations in a public forum. Down the line, who knows who will be reading your email. If you wouldn't say it in a public space (such as an office), don't write it in an email.

12. Use emails as audit trails. If agreeing to arrangements, having an email of what both parties have agreed to is incredibly helpful to avoid confusion. Set up folders next to your email inbox for each place you provide a service to, and save your emails in there as an audit trail.

13. If you have already got to the point where you have too many emails to even contemplate where to start . . . delete all emails over a month old. Yes, we did just say delete everything! If it's really important, someone will contact you again. And when they do, you won't be too busy reading old emails to respond to them.

Equality and equity

Equality means ensuring that all individuals have the same rights, opportunities and resources, regardless of their background or characteristics. It's about treating people fairly and ensuring they are not discriminated against or disadvantaged based on factors like race, gender or disability.

Equity generally means fairness and impartiality – the quality of being fair and just.

Neither means we should deliver the same service to every person!

Ensuring clients know their rights – for example, under the Mental Capacity Act, they have the right to make their own decisions at 16 – and not disadvantaging some clients through undifferentiated delivery are part of what makes our service fair. We have a duty to be inclusive.

So, if you find yourself developing a habit of repeating the same things with every client, and expecting the same outcomes, take a time-out, reflect and adapt.

 Good read

Equity, Diversity, and Inclusion in Career Development, Ifza Shakoor . . .
Find the link in the *Zone*.

Ethics

Ethical use of different social media and technology platforms?

In recent times there have been questions about the ethical use of different social media platforms. We have both seen friends and family question the use of different platforms in their personal lives, as well as organisations holding similar debates.

One argument is that practitioners shouldn't use platforms that conflict with their ethics if they are run by those they see as corrupt or compromised.

A counter to this is that if the voices that would challenge corruption leave the given platform, then there is no challenge or dissent to those who hold extreme views.

The debate goes deeper though and cuts to the heart of practice.

The proliferation of social media and chatbots which can drive content and amplify specific voices or opinions, as well as drive traffic to the various platforms, has laid bare the post-truth world we find ourselves in. It can make it difficult in some settings to separate out the human voices from the noise, and fact from fiction.

It's not just within social media platforms that we are exposed to risk. The very search algorithms we use are not 'search neutral'; depending on how they are set up, they can provide very different results from the same search, with built-in bias.

AI-based tools take this to another level, depending on what source media has been used to develop them, and there are concerns around inherent bias built into some systems.

Identifying and understanding this bias isn't easy.

Within a recent discussion with fellow career practitioners nationally, it was easy to see the uncertainty within ourselves of how to identify bias but also the ethical dilemma of whether to use certain messaging and search platforms or not.

Some tools are independent of the leading multinational search platforms, whereas others piggyback off the big names but, on a cursory look, seem independent.

There remains the dilemma of choosing whether to use certain search tools.

For example, a more sophisticated search tool may lead to more detailed and/or accurate information, which can benefit our clients. Yet in doing so, it may break a personal ethical code if you disagree with the corporation behind the tool you are using. As with all things involving ethics, the answers aren't easy and are very personal.

What does this mean for practice?
An initial answer is that it is currently for each of us to decide on our own ethical positions regarding whether we use one search tool over another.

Yet we have a responsibility to our clients to understand and take ownership of the nuance around these issues, undertaking CPD (Continual Professional Development) so we can take ownership of this; to be informed.

We should have an awareness of the inherent bias in different platforms or through misuse, or clumsy use, of tools which may distort the search results.

The situation isn't static; it is an ever-evolving picture.

Last year Chris was doing some searches for past vlogs he had made while some of the (then new) AI assisted search platforms were launching. He found that old, out-of-date information was rising to the surface from the bottom of the internet.

It was only his personal knowledge of events which allowed him to discern that the information wasn't accurate.

In the same way, our professional curiosity and desire help us to stay on top of fluctuations in the careers sphere within different job roles. Our same curiosity is desirable in understanding the tools we use, and how they are changing, so we aren't passive spectators within the changing landscape.

It is vital in careers practice to pass on how to discern and analyse information for accuracy and validity to our clients. These are the very skills needed for survival in an information and data-driven world.

Ethics

> **Authors' note**
>
> A student was trying to weigh up their choices and was looking at two different sources of career information.
>
> Both described the job they were considering in different ways, with contradictions in the training pathways and different terminology.
>
> On the surface, both were reliable sources from respectable organisations.
>
> Working with the client, Chris discussed what could be the next step.
>
> Initially the client explored other sources of information online but found these to be less reliable and even more out of date.
>
> The client reasoned that talking to someone employed in the role and undertaking work experience would be the most effective way of gaining a better understanding.
>
> While doing so, speaking to someone who oversaw the training within this particular role to gain an understanding of what the situation was locally (where they would be working and training – all being well).
>
> Discussing the situation afterwards, Chris and the client agreed that the ability to research and sift conflicting information sources isn't just important for careers research but in all walks of life . . . from buying a house or car through to understanding the news and politics.
>
> These are skills for life.

A search for 'how to find the inherent bias in different search tools' brings up a plethora of articles which are all good starting points for CPD and wider reading. We have listed some for you to have a look at in our *Zone* at the end of the book.

Many of these focus on the use of search tools, rather than AI chatbots.

It is fair to say the rate of change and sophistication of AI tools go beyond the surface we have skimmed here (indeed, a deep dive into this arena would fill a whole series of books) yet the basic principles of how to check information validity, which many of us were taught during training to become career professionals, remain the same.

Whether we are looking at books, web browsers or AI-led chatbots, when we delve into the minefield of trying to ascertain whether we can trust our sources or not, a back-to-basics approach still stands.

It may be challenging, but do take time to stop and consider to what extent you trust the sources and tools you are using. Making an audit and reflecting on the results is a worthwhile activity for any careers practitioner.

> **Authors' note**
>
> It will probably come as no surprise that Chris loved history at school (and still does). One of his favourite teachers was his history teacher who taught Chris not only how to weigh up and evaluate sources but also how to write and structure an essay.
>
> The principles he learnt in his history classes many years ago still align with how we analyse information sources and the tools we use with clients today.

What can we take as the core principles for practice?

- Check the source – is it trustworthy? Is there a known (publicly acknowledged) bias or record of being fallible?
- What is the date stamp of the information? How recent is it?
- Why was it produced? For what purpose? Is there an inherent agenda?
- When was it last updated? By whom? What are their credentials?
- Is it a primary or secondary source?
- Can the facts be checked against another source?

The issue of ethical practice and trust goes beyond just the search results of the tools we use. It extends to how we practise and how the organisations we work for behave, whether they stick by their values or not when challenged; this in turn affects us and how we are perceived by both customers and clients.

Trust is a fragile thing which can be easily lost once squandered. A deep dive into philosophy brings clarity to the concept.

A related thread which is worth reflecting on are the various theories relating to the 'dead internet' (where a multitude of AI bots are talking to each other and more sinister profiles for hire) through to the concept that eventually the internet will kill itself as no one will know what to believe. One expert recently suggested that we will return to using books more as they are more likely to have been checked for accuracy and validity.

The late great Terry Pratchett (of Discworld fame) even predicted the rise of fake news online in 1995 in an interview with Bill Gates for GQ. (Link to the article in the *Zone*)

He understood the parity stories can hold, whether fact or fiction, and the risk the internet holds in granting parity of esteem, especially when trying to understand what is accurate.

There is a similarity with regard to careers information, as the great AI churn brings up sources from years ago (now outdated) or brings forth the more subtle issue of careers information from other countries that are accurate but relate to their systems, rather than the UK.

We must be wiser and more awake than ever to the ease at which mistakes can be made.

Unethical practice

It is easy to forget in the moment of helping our clients that we are in a role of service, with the responsibilities that this entails to professionalism, ethics and duty.

We need to be mindful of this in case we are faced with being asked to engage in unethical practice. Whether this is massaging figures for reports or being asked by others to direct clients to specific provision, whether by directive practice, omission of choices or through colluding with systematic bias.

To have the confidence to confront and change things when faced with such situations is challenging but can be done if we have the courage of our convictions.

Authors' note

Chris has been placed in several situations in the past where the senior leadership in schools he has visited have challenged him on providing guidance on 'all the options' to the young people in the schools, or he has been asked to provide 10-minute one-to-one sessions to 'tick the box'. This has resulted, on some occasions, in Chris walking away, handing back contracts (with support from his employer) rather than breaching our ethics.

What we do isn't a tick-box exercise; the ethics matter.

Both of us have had robust debates with senior leadership in settings on occasion. In each case, the outcome was similar – a change of view by the Senior Leadership Team (SLT), us being invited in to deliver CPD to staff teams on why career work matters, and a rethink about the structuring of their own provision.

At no point has it resulted in tempers flaring. Just a quiet commitment to our ethics and making time for informed discussion where needed.

We are fortunate to have the backing of employers committed to ethical practice.

Yet what do you do if this isn't the case? Your job may be at risk if you don't follow such requests from senior leadership. A glib answer is to say just walk away and get a new job. But what if you can't get a new job and have bills to pay, people to feed? It's not so easy.

In such scenarios, it takes an awful lot of courage to debate, challenge or disagree with senior leadership. It is understandable if we choose not to take a stand.

If we decide to act, there are practical things which can be done including leaning into the CDI and AGCAS Code of Ethics, as well as the relevant statutory guidance which relates to our settings.

Arming ourselves with information and presenting our case to our SLT, with regard to the importance of impartial, independent guidance (without external or enforced agendas) matters for our clients.

Changing the debate to the language of those we are presenting to, explaining why not being independent is a business risk (if being inspected or similar) is another tactic we can take.

Finding allies in the setting who may support us, such as alternative members of senior leadership, can also be useful as they may be able to carry the debate to others in senior positions if we are in more junior positions.

Discussing and seeking support from a network of peers and/or supervision is worthwhile for our mental health so that we aren't alone with the situation.

It's good to talk.

Agendafication (a made-up word meaning to embrace a particular ideology or position)

There are so many different agendas that seek to hijack or derail the client-centred nature of careers work, including the ones inside our own heads. We have explored how important it is to disclose any kind of agenda to our clients; to remain client-centred.

Agendafication leads to the risk of a systematic or widespread shift within a careers programme or the wider careers sphere itself.

Examples include the promotion of one set of occupations (such as STEM or STEAM) or ways of being over another . . . or to the exclusion of other positions or ways of being.

Over the years we have seen many industry bodies engage with careers advisers to encourage them to promote their particular sector, with the argument being that it is in the clients' best interests.

Yet what does this really mean?

Is it in their best economic or mental health interests? Or is it rather the interests of the professional body or interest group?

However . . . opportunity awareness is an important aspect of careers work alongside self-awareness.

Our own professional agenda is often to ensure students have all their options; this in itself is a position (or 'agenda') for careers work.

In our roles, we may be in a position of responsibility to invite others into our venues, to give talks and raise awareness.

To actively promote one type of job over another veers into agendafication, moving beyond the principles of independence, which guidance holds dear.

Travelling around the country, we have seen settings where the majority of talks are from Higher Education Institutions; the other options just simply don't get a look in.

We have seen situations where the only talks are from professionals; those who are traditionally from a trade background don't appear. There is a distinct difference between 'raising aspirations' and 'widening aspirations'; the former takes a hierarchical position whereas the latter speaks loudly of opening up all possibilities.

How we shape our career programmes matters. If we weigh all our resources towards one or two pathways, it is no surprise when clients only take those routes rather than the pathways they have heard less about or had less support to access.

For reference, typical Post-18 options (dependent on qualifications and experience) in England are currently (at the time of writing) as follows:

- Apprenticeships (including foundation apprenticeships and degree apprenticeships);
- Higher Education – bachelor's and integrated master's degrees, HNDs, HNCs, foundation degrees, HTQs;
- Colleges – FE, sixth form and independent specialist provision;
- Supported employment/internships;

- Distance learning (HE), possibly alongside work and/or volunteering;
- Online learning (e.g. Alison and MOOC courses) combined with work and/or travel and/or volunteering;
- Work-based training (non-apprenticeship), for example, to secure an SIA licence for security guards;
- Gap year/gap term – for travel and/or mental health break and/or to earn money for Higher Education;
- Work;
- Volunteering (with or without training);
- Entrepreneurship/own business;
- Community-based activities and support such as day centres, self-directed support options and residential care.

 Insider tip

We need to ask ourselves – are all our talks or interactions only focused on one or two options, or do ALL the other options get a look in?

Everyone has a right to career guidance

How many times we've both been told that a client doesn't need career guidance because . . .

- They've already decided.
- They won't be seeking work.
- They won't talk.
- They don't have mental capacity.

Our job is to help people be as involved in their own choices and decision-making as much as possible.

We are trained to facilitate communication. We are trained to help people find the best way for them to make choices. We are trained to open up possibilities and coach people in the skills they will need to make those possibilities happen.

Don't worry that you aren't 'intelligent' enough to support the A* students and polymaths. We have our own specific type of intelligence. We are experts in career thinking. Your clients may be super intelligent, but equally, they are still just people who get lost, stuck and tied in knots about their future; they need our care and guidance.

Everyone has a right to career guidance!

If you want to explore inclusive practice within career development, have a read of our first book – *Career Development and Inclusive Practice*.

F

Find your tribe

Employability coaches and career professionals
For as long as there have been CDPs, there have been employability coaches, advisers, mentors or assistants; these roles are just as crucial in the world of careers as that of CDPs.

We love these associates within the careers sphere.

One of Chris' mentors, Malcolm, recalls the early days of his work in the careers service. The service with young people looked more akin to what we see as the work of JobCentres in England (note: his recollections of these days can be found on Chris' personal YouTube channel).

In those days, Malcolm recalled working with career assistants in his career in the 1980s, who were similar in many ways to the employability roles that many services employ today.

He recalls their job was to support careers officers by preparing the 'units' or information files before school interviews, preparing any information or handout requirements, filing the units by school, registering clients once they had left school and registered as unemployed, placing clients into work, apprenticeship or youth training schemes and maintaining careers libraries and vacancy boards. Before he started, they also distributed unemployment benefits to clients. Many of them went on to become Careers Officers/Consultants/Advisers once the part-time training route was established.

Recognising and nurturing this talent pipeline, especially in today's challenging time, is crucial.

Chris began his own career in careers in a support role. In the early days of his career, he started as a Student Mentor in 2002, as one of the first pastoral support staff in the FE sector (before this, many colleges relied on their academic teachers to support with pastoral needs).

It was under the auspices of the legendary Pru Blackwell that Chris developed his early career, as he navigated his first steps in education. Pru (now retired) went on to run a careers service for young people in East Sussex.

Chris looks back on those early days of his career with fondness; he later trained to be a teacher and became a personal tutor for the art school, which was part of the college.

Although at the time not 'qualified' in careers he supported students with UCAS applications and engaged them in discussions on their next steps and thoughts about the future, in a similar way to how many Career Leaders and Employability Assistants do in schools and colleges today.

Looking back, Chris remembers how much he enjoyed connecting with students and helping them but recognises that there was a lot he was naive about and didn't know.

These roles helped him to test out what he wanted to do, with a later pivot away from teaching towards careers.

Students he supported at college have contacted him over the years and, from their feedback, his support was appreciated as they journeyed on their way. In his early days in careers, Chris also worked with Intensive Careers Advisers who provided follow-up support from career sessions in community venues, helping with personal needs and job applications. Due to this and the acknowledgement of the benefits to society these roles provide, Chris retains a soft spot for those working in similar roles, from colleagues at CXK today who do an amazing job, through to the 'Designated Staff Members' (DSMs) he met at local universities recently; these pastoral and career support roles matter.

We need to guard against the tendency to demonise employability coaches and assistants; sometimes coming from a lack of knowledge and training and sometimes done as a misguided way of bolstering our own professional identity by putting others down, or as a well-intentioned self-defence to protect the professionalism of careers.

In this context, CDPs recognise the professionalism, knowledge and understanding of career development models and theories which underpin what we do. However, we also should recognise the many amazing employability coaches and similar (who are 'unqualified') that do an amazing job day in and day out, and who are worth celebrating and championing in their own right.

We see you and support you! We think you are fab!

It may be that you are reading this in such a role and wish to take your 'career in careers' further, but you are unsure how to do so.

Caroline Green (The Talent Cycle) and John Paley (Resourceful Careers) have produced a resource to help navigate the various 'careers in careers' across the sector.

You'll find a link to *'Careers in Careers – Your Guide to a Career that Changes Lives'* in the *Zone*. It is well worth a look if you are in an employability or pastoral role and wish to explore what is possible or are looking to enter the sector.

Trust circle

We all need people around us whom we trust – to help us reflect and to bring out the best in us.

When you are establishing a trust circle for yourself in the careers sphere, consider:

- What do you bring?
- What/who do you need?
- Other CDPs with differing views, skills and approaches make for great learning.

- Other professionals play a vital role in helping young people develop career-thinking brains – they can bring a welcome new perspective.
- Senior leaders have a different view of careers as a business. Is this something you want to learn about?
- Parents and carers have a particular view of career guidance in relation to their children – how are you supported by these views in your role?
- Who do you trust to give you feedback about negative experiences without you feeling simply criticised?
- Clients are not always clients – do you have/want people with lived experience in your circle?
- Do you have trust in your circle? If you don't trust someone, you won't be able to share safely and grow.
- People can be a positive part of your working life without them being part of your trust circle.

You may be fortunate enough to have professional guidelines, yearly observations and regular line management and/or supervision to discuss, explore and develop practice.

For those who have their own businesses, work freelance or are isolated in their role, joining a community of practitioners can be useful not only for emotional support but also for practical support via peer observations.

The CDI has a useful set of resources to support observations and self-reflection – we've put a link in the *Zone*.

Joining professional networks (whether the local CDI networks or more informal groups online or in person) can be a huge help for practice.

Some groups charge a membership fee and may focus on a particular area of the careers sphere (such as the Careers Writers Association – which Chris currently chairs), whereas others are looser collectives, such as the 'fuddles' organised across the country by the legendary Liane Hambly and Katherine Jennick.

These networks help to challenge us, support our emotional wellbeing and can be used to explore matters of practice at a philosophical level.

Careers coordinators come and go

Careers Leaders are a relatively new role within schools – organising and coordinating career activities across their school.

Building a partnership with your Careers Leader in school can pay dividends.

Some career practitioners in school will also be the Careers Leader (in which case it should be straightforward to build a partnership with yourself, lol). In other settings, such as prisons and universities, there are similar roles and people who we need to partner with to develop a successful service.

Building a partnership, rather than just working together, is useful not only for clients but also for ourselves, as partnerships in their truest sense are relationships which are defined by openness . . . including being able to call each other out on things, give and take constructive feedback, and consider how things can be improved. Partnerships are also incredibly useful for emotional support and wellbeing.

So how do we build partnerships?

Generally, it is the same as how we build relationships with our clients: active listening and making time for each other. In many settings, this can be challenging, so actively taking time to sit down and discuss things is important.

Whether for just debriefing on the day or sharing concerns that have arisen, taking this time matters.

But partnerships change and evolve. Over the years, both of us have built up partnerships with key staff in our respective settings, only to see them leave or be promoted into senior leadership roles . . . leaving us to build relationships with new staff. Such is the way of things.

Being open to this churn and change, although wearing at times, isn't something to be fought. Rather, it is something to embrace (like getting older!). Out of these changes, sometimes exciting things can happen.

 Authors' note

For example, one of the Careers Leaders Chris worked with for years is now a headteacher at a new school. He completely understands careers and, from when his new school opened, he had Chris coming in to deliver targeted careers work to his Year 7s (something which is fairly rare); the reason for this was partly down to the strength of the relationship Chris and he built over the years when they worked together at another school. Thanks, Jon!

There are numerous other occasions where the relationships we have built earlier in our careers have come back and been supportive later in our career journeys (often in different settings or contexts).

The careers sphere is a small world – work on your partnerships within it and celebrate their success.

 Insider tips

If you look after your settings, your settings will look after you in times of change and/or uncertainty.

Don't park in the boss's car parking space.

Make friends with the ICT technician, caretaker and receptionist wherever you work . . . they are the gatekeepers to sacred knowledge and will make your life easier when you are stuck, locked in or lost!

Pick your battles.

We live and die by our reputations; the careers sphere is much smaller than we may realise! If we gossip, or aren't genuine, our reputation will go before us. Likewise, if we are known for fantastic client-centred practice, this too will go before us.

Build partnerships. Careers guidance is best when not conducted in a vacuum. We need partners to help our clients. When we work together to support our clients, magic happens.

Disability, health conditions, identity and being a CDP

We know a few CDPs who have disabilities, health conditions and/or spicy brains (as the popular colloquialism goes).

Since writing our first book on Inclusive Guidance (published by Trotman), which explores how to support clients with impairments, health conditions and learning support needs within a careers guidance context, we have been contacted by numerous careers practitioners who have had these experiences themselves.

We were humbled by how many said that not only did their clients feel seen due to the previous book, but they also felt seen as neurodivergent and/or disabled practitioners in their multitude of different ways of being.

As one of our friends would say . . . 'at times we are a complicated hot mess, but we are here and we are loud'.

For years, Chris struggled with his identity, feeling like he didn't fit in and was 'too much'. At times celebrated and at other times ostracised for his eccentricity (as he calls it). Although being compared to a certain chap who travels through time and space, as well as a wizard, was fun, it was only through finding unconditional acceptance at work (in addition to friends and family) that he has been able to come to value himself. Yet we are aware that not everywhere, or everyone, is as accepting of difference.

We can only speak from our lived experiences and those of colleagues and friends.

Through this, we have come to realise that many others who faced (and sadly still face) discrimination over the years have been struggling in isolation.

Friends who are LGBTQIA+, from different ethnic groups, disabled or have health conditions, have faced some horrible forms of discrimination over the years.

We take the time, here and now, to say this is not acceptable in the careers sphere.

If faced with discrimination, or struggling with work due to health conditions or disability, don't struggle on your own. We've put some organisations in the *Zone* to give you a place to start.

Chris was fortunate at his place of work that he was able to receive support. Through understanding his own conditions, he has also been able to utilise strategies to enable him to thrive: from using whiteboards to structuring his time and duties to align with how his mind works. However, we are aware that it isn't as easy for everyone, and especially for those with complicated and/or lifelong conditions which involve chronic pain and/or fatigue.

As for discrimination, its insidious nature is something we must guard against. Not just for ourselves but also for our friends, colleagues and clients. Each of us sets the tone for what the careers sphere is and what it may become.

Culture is defined and dictated by everyone in a group, acting together. It is not defined by a few individuals. We are all responsible for what we become as a profession.

We hope it is one defined by peace, mutual respect, tolerance, acceptance and kindness.

This is who we are.

Future gazing

We have looked to the past and considered the top tips from previous years. How might 'careers work' change and evolve in the next twenty years? How might we prepare for this?

Speculative crystal ball gazing is always dangerous, as the future we inherit isn't the one we always expect.

National and regional variations make it difficult to predict.

For example, about ten years ago the narrative of technology rapidly taking over jobs was the order of the day. Chris can remember talk of accountants being out of work within two years following a Deloitte report[1] . . . and there was a blip. Chris observed what seemed to be the start of a fall in the number of accountants and bookkeepers, as some companies dallied with technology-based processes, reducing their finance teams in turn.

Yet a year or so later, fortunes reversed.

Kent (where Chris is based) is approximately 80% SMEs (small and medium-sized enterprise)[2] – it seemed that these businesses still needed their accountants and bookkeepers, despite the predictions of their demise.

Looking at the Labour Market Information (LMI) today, financial and accountancy-related occupations remain within the top ten of the highest paying jobs in the county.[3]

However, if you clicked on the link in five years' time, could we say the same?

We write this in a world where Deloitte and others are taking far fewer graduates and apprentices for their trainee programmes.[4]

We aren't intending to take a deep dive into the economics and signs of the times; instead, these thoughts are an observation that what we think we know will happen doesn't always happen. In many instances, we are oblivious to the warnings or signs of change on the horizon.

When Chris was first training (before Connexions funding cuts) his colleague and friend Malcolm had described how, over about 30 years, he had worked

---

1 https://www.ifac.org/knowledge-gateway/discussion/exploring-artificial-intelligence-accountancy-profession-opportunity-threat-both-neither
2 https://www.kentbusinessradio.co.uk/small-business-stats
3 https://www.adzuna.co.uk/jobs/salaries/kent
4 https://www.cityam.com/big-four-slash-graduate-jobs-as-ai-takes-on-entry-level-work

for lots of different organisations, while generally remaining in the same few schools as a Careers Adviser.

One of the other careers advisers who had been around for a while, on hearing this, remarked how foolhardy and unlikely it would be for the government to cut funding for careers. Funding sources might change but 'careers work would always be a safe job' was their prevailing wisdom. 'It would be political suicide to cut the funding' was one comment. Yet, the cuts to careers came (in England), and they ran deep ... with approximately 80% of CDPs losing or changing jobs.

Malcolm had remarked before this that as long as you kept some face-to-face delivery, change was something CDPs were more likely to be able to weather; however, the sector was, and will remain, volatile due to its political nature.

Both of us have continued to do face-to-face delivery while in management roles. In addition to the fact that we both love working with clients, this gives us first-hand experience of how the changing landscape is affecting our clients and our colleagues. And it keeps our guidance skills honed.

Technology such as AI is gaining pace, against an increasingly volatile socio-economic and political backdrop.

We're not going to land any predictions here of what might happen in the future (as they are very likely to be wrong), but we may wish to ponder and reflect upon what the future could hold:

- Does what we love about our work remain, or has what we love about the calling of careers work changed?
- Do we practise in the same way we used to? What has changed and what has stayed the same?
- What is worth pulling forward in time from the past? Conversely, what is worth leaving in the past?
- What technological changes have transformed/are transforming our day-to-day lives?
- If you were building a careers service from scratch (without prior knowledge) how would you set it up? Would you do what you do now? What would you do differently?

G

Going places

Before you set off:

- Make sure you know if Sat Nav will actually take you to the setting! There are some settings where Sat Nav doesn't cut it. A quick call to the setting in the week before you are due to go there can give you invaluable information about landmarks, parking, whether you need to take your DBS with you, do you need a packed lunch and so on . . .

When you first arrive at a new setting:

- Along with signing-in arrangements, knowing where the fire assembly point is, where the toilets, staff room and tea/coffee facilities are is important. These are the practical day-to-day things that can make your days go so much smoother and although quite mundane, remain practical considerations. Especially knowing where the tea and coffee is!
- Make sure you know where the kettle and toilets are.

The Career Development Professional's Survival Guide

- Make sure your bag of 'stuff' isn't too heavy – it is tempting to try and take lots of resources with us, but make sure yours suits you and your circumstances.
- And each time you start in a new setting, make sure you do your own risk assessment.

H

Have a go!

We can't all be great at everything immediately . . . but if we don't give it a go, we may never find out what works for us and for our clients.

- Experiment;
- Diversify;
- Extend your 'toolkit';
- Put all sorts of career theories into practice;
- Try working with a client group you haven't encountered previously;
- Observe other people to see how they do things differently;
- Take part in experiential activities;
- Move the chairs round;
- Try walking and talking;
- Challenge yourself to move out of your comfort zone.

For the first few years of his practice, Chris was terrified of public speaking, assemblies and group work. He would try and try to deliver as his mentors in both careers (and before this, teaching) did.

When he was a teacher, and as a trainee Careers Adviser, each time he felt things fell flat and didn't fly as he thought they would. The more he tried to be a 'professional' and be like the others around him, the worse the delivery was.

Ultimately, when organising a careers delivery in a school, he would persuade the school not to have any assemblies or group sessions (so he could avoid them); they terrified him. Too much was going on (for his then not-understood ADHD brain and related anxiety).

Then the funding changes hit.

Anything and everything was given a go to just keep going (organisations were falling by the wayside rapidly in England as the cuts hit).

Chris' manager booked Chris in for a delivery which was (unbeknown to him at the time) pivotal for his development.

A whole year group assembly, 200 or so students and Chris – looking at Post-16 options for one hour.

Initially, Chris was terrified (feeling physically sick), yet he said OK when asked. He went away and thought about things, reflecting on what he could do.

He had the epiphany that he needed to stop thinking about 'being an anxious person' and remember what the work was about . . . the clients. He thought to himself – if I was a young person, what would I need from an hour's session?

What would different young people need?

This led to him devising an assembly which involved variety, props and activities which were interactive and engaged the students. Climbing rope, nerf guns and superhero masks were the order of the day! He stopped delivering like others and delivered in a way which was true to himself.

On the day of this assembly he used a tennis ball (which he bounced, like a metronome) to regulate his ADHD at the start.

He also took off the suit jacket he was wearing, literally rolled up his sleeves and went for it . . . In doing so, he became himself.

> If you aren't a fan of group work yourself, try shadowing some colleagues who do it well. Group engagement in careers activities offers scope to develop career-thinking skills and behaviours that 1:1 interventions don't. And if you're using it to do introductions, clarify expectations and so on . . . it will also save you time and increase the likelihood that clients will positively engage with you.

Jules used to avoid using art as part of her practice – there is a reason why it is Chris that does the illustrations for the books! However, a fantastic mentor encouraged Jules to use drawing and visual tools for the benefit of clients who process better visually. Now Jules uses loads of art and visuals in her work. She is still pretty rubbish at drawing! However, this has the added bonus of redressing the power imbalance within interventions. Clients recognise that they are better at some things than Jules is and take ownership of the artwork that forms part of their action plan.

Just to prove that we can all 'have a go', Jules has contributed some artwork for this book.

 Insider tips

Have backup props or visuals for when technology fails.

Keep practising (it is called careers practice for a reason).

The day you think you know everything is the day you are dangerous and should walk away. What you put in is what you get out.

Stay playful as part of creative, inclusive practice.

Have fun!

Don't panic!

Humour

To joke or not to joke, that is the question.

And it's a tricky one.

Humour is beneficial. It helps to improve morale and cohesion. However, it is easy for jokes, intentionally or not, to go too far, be interpreted the wrong way or simply be offensive.

This can lead to grievances or even tribunal cases.

Recent case law has made clear that where workplace 'banter' oversteps the mark it can amount to unlawful discrimination, typically harassment, in cases where comments make reference to the 'protected characteristics' under the Equality Act 2010.

So, think before you joke. And be clear that you are joking.

I

Information sharing

As part of our Code of Ethics, confidentiality is key. However, for most clients, their personal support network is important in helping them take their plans to fruition.

For many students who have learning support needs, their network is going to be vital in enabling them to succeed.

This awareness builds on not only community interaction theory by Bill Law, which discusses where our ideas come from and who influences them, but also the Systems Theory Framework of Careers Development by McMahon and Patton.

So how do we 'square the circle?'

For us, it is a question of building consent into the sessions, of what we will share, with whom and how. There are many different ways to do this (Chris uses the Open Partnership Model which he co-authored – see the *Zone*), but it is your choice as to what method works best for you.

Some colleagues weave this sometimes-tricky element into their contracting using 'flash cards' or 'posters' which are prepared as prompts for discussion.

However you choose to weave it in, it is important to consider the use of language which is used and that it is appropriate and understandable (without being patronising) by the client group you are working with.

If you use the word 'confidential' as part of your discussion, check that the client knows what it means by asking them what they think it means.

If they struggle with verbal communication, ask them to point to prepared cards with simplified definitions on. Have some examples ready.

What many of us will say is that we won't share what is discussed with anyone else without permission, unless it affects the health and safety of the client or others (and then discuss/provide an example).

It is worth expanding this to include action plans and a discussion about what is produced, how and with whom it is shared.

Some of this might be included in pre-session information you have provided or sent to the client beforehand but, even if this is the case, it is worth 'checking-in' with the client and discussing, so the understanding is explicit (rather than implicit).

We don't just want 'consent'; we are after 'enthusiastic consent'.

Doing this protects against any issues which may arise later (such as clients not wanting to share information with others).

It is an approach which is embedded in our commitment to transparent practice and professional ethics.

Pre-session information

Pre-session information can include a variety of things, such as how the session is delivered, by whom and how.

In some of our schools and colleges we:

- Provide a bespoke video for our clients to watch before we come in. This tackles two aspects: one being a clear explanation of what we do and how we work, the other helping to reduce anxiety and worry that clients may face in meeting an unknown adult or stranger.
- Take a hybrid approach and embed information on their website with a change in language to make things more inclusive.
- Provide worksheets and/or infographics/posters which explain our service in a simplified manner to help prepare students.
- Provide plasma-screen slides (which play as part of the loop on the numerous plasma-screens in school). These cover what we do, how we work and a 'fun fact' for each adviser in the school; they are easy to make using PowerPoint software and very effective in not only promoting our services but also explaining what we do (demystifying 'careers') and preparing learners.

We've put some examples for you in the *Zone*.

Sharing action plans

Sharing an action plan with a lead professional (such as the SENCO or personal tutor) in a school or college (and having an ongoing dialogue with them) is important so that they can build the client's wishes into their transition plans.

It can also be useful as a sense check, as the client (due to their needs) might not be as aware of issues or situations that may impact their next steps.

The same can be true of sharing information with the parents or carers who are supporting the clients.

Such sharing of information to ensure clients are supported requires a delicate approach and consideration, especially if there is friction with others in their network (whether members of staff in a school or college, or even with family members).

> ### Who decides?
>
> - The decision-making rights of young people over the age of 16 are subject to whether they have capacity under the Mental Capacity Act 2005 (MCA). There is an assumption that a young person has capacity unless there is a reasonable belief that they do not, at which point an assessment of capacity should take place.
> - Mental capacity is assessed in relation to the particular decision which needs to be made (in this case, who to share the action plan with). This means that whether a young person has the mental capacity to make a particular decision or not has to be considered on an individual basis in the light of the circumstances at the time.
> - We should always start with a presumption of capacity.
> - We have a duty to support individuals to make their own decisions.
> - People are allowed to make unwise choices!
> - When we are trying to decide whether a child or young person <u>under the age of 16</u> is mature enough to make decisions for themselves, we refer to Gillick Competence, which is based on a child being able to understand a decision, what it involves and to retain the information and communicate their decision.

Discussing with clients how 'sharing with others' can be built into their careers support is important in providing clients with the autonomy, agency and ownership of their own lives and actions. It should not be assumed that information will be shared with teachers or support staff and that 'careers support' is something which is 'done to' them rather than with them.

This is crucial if the action plan will form part of the discussions at an annual or transitional review with other professionals and family members present.

> 'No decision about me, without me'

Consider this within the context of career guidance – and in particular where we are working with students who have learning support needs and/or are disabled.

We often find that support is at risk of following the 'medical model of disability' rather than the social model, which can affect how support and discussions around next steps potentially develop for our clients.

The social model is arguably congruent with our client-centred approach which places the client at the centre of our interactions and support.

The medical model suggests that people are disabled because of impairments or conditions that they have. This implies that the problem is with the disabled person.

The social model recognises that from a disabled person's perspective, the problems they face are the barriers created by society. Assuming that a disabled person 'can't do' something creates a barrier for that person.

An approach which builds upon and recognises the social model of disability isn't a guarantee of success but is potentially one which is fairer and places the client at the centre of the work we do.

It is a model we must listen and attend to:

'The social model of disability is a way of thinking about disability, created by disabled people.'

However, there is a risk that a client can be 'in the room' but still have decisions made about them, and for them, without their views being taken into consideration; being 'superficially inclusive'.

Career Development Professionals have a valuable role to play as advocates, to ensure that the client's voice is heard, is given equal weight to the professionals and family members in attendance, and is actively seen as being the most valuable.

Information Sharing

It is vital that their decisions are informed, which is where high-quality careers guidance comes in. We need to ensure that clients:

- have the space for careers support;
- have time and support to understand the options and possibilities available to them;
- explore what is important to them.

It is crucial that their CDP has the tools, as well as the professional skills and training, to deliver careers guidance in a way which is accessible and inclusive; ensuring that it is not only meaningful but also worthwhile.

Part of our agreement with our clients at the start of the session is about ensuring that the client's voice is heard with active consent as to how we will work together.

It is important to explore whether the client is happy to share their action plan with education providers, parents or carers and for them to have agency over what is written on it.

For most clients this isn't an issue. However, a few do raise concerns about what is shared. This can be easily resolved by having some options available:

- Have a separate piece of paper or pre-printed action plan document available.

You can agree to write on this document information that is just for the client, with a typed action plan kept 'for the school' only containing that which the client is happy to share with others.

- Share a generic document for carers, parents and others, which sets out information on the full range of options, places to source careers information and links to quizzes and resources, which is separate from the written record of your individual conversation.
- Discuss what concerns they might have; type the whole action plan up with the client and agree on the wording together so that, when it is shared, they are okay with what has been written.

Both of us usually give an example of the kind of thing we wouldn't expect to put in a plan:

'We can add notes to the action plan during the session. I will then type them up neatly after the session and send them on to your tutor so they can support with your next steps.

'However, if you tell me you don't like your teacher, I won't write it on your action plan. You just tell me the bits you don't want written down.'

Most students give a little chuckle and are completely fine with this.

It is rare for young people to not want their plan shared, but when this does happen, it is easily resolved (using a combination of the approaches detailed above).

It is important to check why the client doesn't wish to share the information with others in case it links with a child protection or safeguarding concern.

J

Just one thing

Too much information, too many questions, too much pressure to make choices can all feel very overwhelming.

If your client seems overwhelmed, or if you are, try doing *Just One Thing*.

Doing just one thing can improve focus, reduce stress and avoid the cognitive strain and distraction of multitasking, allowing your brain to work more efficiently. And when you successfully complete your one thing, your brain gets a dopamine hit which encourages it to do more.

Every decision, every plan, every journey starts with doing just one thing!

K

Kindness

Look after yourself and others – be kind! Costs nothing.

Sustainable practice – mental and physical health

Careers guidance is a wonderful thing, a force for good in an ever more complicated and confusing world. However, it can also be hard work, draining and leave practitioners exhausted, if not practised in a sustainable manner.

The environment(s) we find ourselves in contribute significantly to the extent to which we can create a practice which is both meaningful and sustainable.

There are ways of being, which we can consider to improve our lot:

- Be mindful that we can't help everyone – there are some clients we won't be able to support, no matter how good a practitioner we are.
- You are not everyone's cup of tea – you will not gel with some clients, for reasons which are beyond your control or theirs. This is ok.
- Consider the size and weight of your toolkit – in recent years, there has been a zeitgeist to use more and more props and resources in practice, which is exciting and interesting. However, this can lead to us carrying bags which become cumbersome and heavy. This isn't particularly great for our wellbeing and health if we have to take our resources with us to different settings. Being mindful of what we carry is important; making sure we don't damage our backs with heavy bags.
- Build your toolkit around the clients you are supporting. Don't try and take every prop with you. Consider taking with you only what you need for the day.
- Give yourself a toolkit breather. Remind yourself of what you can do when it is just you, a pen and a pad of paper. Leave the toolkit at home and just take the most basic essentials. This is a way to challenge and reinvigorate your practice. It is a 'creative' challenge in the sense that it reminds you of what you are capable of, beyond the bells and whistles.

Not only will it help you grow in confidence in your practice, but as you realise that you can practise with just who you are, it will help you become more creative in your use of questions. It can help prepare you if there is a moment in the future when you don't have your props, and reduce long-term anxiety, as it stops your props becoming crutches.

- Put emails on mute. Emails can be endless – they keep popping up. This can distract us during practice and act as a stress-inducing niggle. Mute them while supporting clients and only check them when you have time to read and respond to them. Emails are, in our experience, such a challenge that we've given them their own section.
- Recognise when you are unwell or too tired to support. We get sick and we get tired. Many of us are aware of how clients should avoid making decisions when they are sick or tired. We should be mindful of not supporting if we are too tired or sick. In not taking time to recuperate, not only are we not providing a professional service (and are potentially dangerous in the support we may provide), but we are also further putting ourselves at risk (especially if we have to drive or commute while in this state).
- Boundary what you do. Having professional boundaries is important, not only in our relationships with clients and other professionals such as teachers; it is also vital for how we protect ourselves. Working outside of our hours, or allowing all and sundry to pick our brains for 'advice' while not at work, is a fast track way to burn out.

Being too close

This is an aspect of practice which has come up several times in our working lives: when we are too close to the person we are seeking to support to be effective.

Chris and Jules have both had colleagues in careers whose children wouldn't listen to them as their relationship meant the parent was too close to remain impartial and detached enough to offer support.

Having discussed the situation, they recognised they were too close and asked us to see their children as an independent CDP.

It has nothing to do with their own practice; it was just they couldn't create the professional distance they needed for clarity to offer the best support to their child.

What it did mean, once they had trust in a safe and confidential space for their child to talk, was that they could concentrate on their most vital role of being a parent.

If you are seeing friends' or colleagues' children, ensure:

- Everyone knows the boundaries (confidentiality, information sharing etc.).
- The electronic or paper records are not accessible by the parent without explicit permission.
- You feel resilient enough to stick to the boundaries regardless of your friendship or professional relationship.
- You ask an independent colleague for confidential advice or support if it becomes difficult.

There is also a safety issue if we are supporting people outside of the boundaries where we work. For example, if there was a child protection issue or a similar disclosure that required dealing with.

- Give yourself time to switch off and relax. We can't be 'on' all the time. Making the time to embrace hobbies and downtime, to just be, is vital for recharging.
- Allow time for reflection and CPD, but don't let it overwhelm you. Reflection and CPD are important for practice, but the danger is that it can swamp us. With reflective practice, we can get caught in a cycle whereby we get hung up on what we have or haven't done. What we feel we could have done better or done differently. If we are not careful, this can result in overthinking, where we get swamped and can't escape a rabbit hole of thoughts.
- With CPD, the danger is we try and read everything for FOMO (Fear of Missing Out) and end up drowning in too much information. Don't try to keep up with everything, as otherwise you might break. Build your reflective practice around the needs of your client base.
- Celebrate your own successes and recognise when and how practice improves. It is dangerous to rely solely on external validation of what we do. Recognise and see your daily wins and the value the work you do brings, even if no one else sees it. It matters, you matter . . . we see you!
- If you give a client the wrong piece of information or a session 'goes wrong', it isn't the end of the world (we aren't brain surgeons). Follow-on information can be sent to clients and apologies made if required. Don't let mistakes or missteps eat you up.

L

Learning styles

Career guidance is all about learning and communication.

All of us have unique needs when it comes to communication and decision-making.

Think about how we process and use information, explain ideas to our clients and organise our own thoughts.

Each of our brains is not only unique, but what we need to thrive is just as distinctive.

The myth of learning styles?

Many commentators now suggest that we may have preferences with regard to how we learn in different contexts, but not a fixed 'learning style' as this may change depending on what we are learning and where.

Point to ponder: If we approached all students (not just those categorised as having learning support needs) as having unique ways of learning, processing information, making decisions and then attending to these, would the world of education be more egalitarian?

Where do 'learning or additional needs' and 'learning styles or preferences' start and end?

When many people are waiting on a diagnosis or assessment of a learning support need, impairment, learning disability . . . call it what you will . . . and are struggling to have their needs recognised and met, there becomes a tension between what we understand with regards to 'learning styles' and 'learning needs' or 'differences' for those who are disabled by our learning structures and environments.

It is murky, an area of fierce debate, and one which leans into the medical model of disability which requires a diagnosis as a verification of needs or disability.

> If you would like to find out more about models of disability and inclusive practice, please do check out our book *Career Development and Inclusive Practice*.

But getting back to you and your clients . . .

If we, as practitioners, have a preference for thinking in a certain way and are anxious, or struggle to think in different ways, outside of this . . . what does this mean for practice? Especially if our ways of thinking might be different to our clients.

Try asking your clients, 'how do you like your information . . . do you prefer lists, mind maps, paper or websites?'

Mayer and colleagues have extensively studied how students learn with visuals and audio, and the interaction of the two. What he and his colleagues suggest is that providing dual streams of information, in multiple formats, engages learners to work harder at understanding the material, which leads to better learning.

It may be that the research on learning styles is actually showing that teaching with different modalities is just more interesting to students rather than catering to a particular style of learning.[1]

'The best learning takes place when an individual can connect and incorporate information into his or her personal experiences and understanding.'[2]

What does it mean when our brains work differently to our clients in a client-centred practice, such as careers counselling?

The practitioners' needs, as well as the clients', are important – working in an open partnership.

---

1 Krätzig, G. P., & Arbuthnott, K. D. (2006). Perceptual learning style and learning proficiency: A test of the hypothesis. *Journal of Educational Psychology, 98*(1), 238–246. https://doi.org/10.1037/0022-0663.98.1.238

2 https://hechingerreport.org/how-scrapping-the-one-size-fits-all-education-defeats-inequity

We should use approaches that:

- both client and practitioner are comfortable with;
- are within our professional competencies and boundaries;
- are engaging and provided via different modalities to improve learning and understanding.

As professionals, we can reflect on where we struggle and look to improve our abilities – and extend our comfort zone – in these areas to provide the best possible service to our clients.

How our minds work, and how we learn, remain an area of ongoing research and debate. Being open to these changing concepts and ideas is an important part of the career practitioner's professional curiosity.

Looking after the planet

Sustainable Practice – 'green' guidance

In the 'careers sphere' some commentators have spoken about 'green guidance' as part of a wider agenda, as part of social justice. Putting the potential agendafication of careers work to one side, it is worth our taking the time to consider a different angle on what this can mean for careers practice and sustainability.

From one perspective, there is a call to help clients grow their understanding of how they can contribute to a more sustainable ('greener') world. Yet, to what extent do we, individually and collectively, take responsibility for how our own profession contributes to a 'greener' world?

Do we use resources in our toolkits which are reusable or disposable? Do we embrace methods which are more in harmony with the world?

 Authors' note

A few years ago, Chris was reflecting on his practice and realised that he was using lots and lots of whiteboard pens in his practice (using whiteboards for 'Career Mapping' activities). He switched to reusable whiteboard pens which, initially, are more expensive than standard pens but use cartridges that can be recycled and the pens reused with fresh cartridges; this has drastically reduced his waste (if you go on the CXK YouTube channel – links in the *Zone* – you can watch a video where he discusses this).

He went further and bought some playing card sized mini whiteboards which are reusable (wipe clean) to use instead of sticky notes (that often get thrown in the bin afterwards). At CXK the team switched to using digital action plans where possible (emailing these to clients). Where not possible (such as within group guidance), clients use manual or paper action plans which are pre-printed on sustainably sourced paper.

An area which is contentious, and possibly overlooked, is that of AI. From an environmental perspective, the impact of using AI within careers research can be seen as problematic. Recent studies indicate that AI searches use more power than traditional search engines . . . they're consuming more power and natural resources, such as water, to keep data-centres cool. There is the cumulative impact of the components required in the electronics and the data-centres; the extent to which they utilise new (rather than recycled) resources and whether they draw their power from renewable sources rather than fossil fuels.

Looking after The Planet

Yet the flipside is how useful and helpful AI may be in our work. Imagine the social good that can be achieved if using AI helps our clients identify opportunities, find secure employment or enter roles that help improve the world, making it a better place.

It is not a zero-sum game of being all good or all bad.

What does this mean for us?

If we are concerned about our wider impact on the world, it is worth us considering what small changes we can make in our own practice that will make the world a 'greener' place.

Small changes can build up to big impacts. By changing our daily habits, we can have an impact on the individual footprint that we leave in the world.

This can be from using more renewable resources in our practice to having conversations with those we work for and with to influence the green initiatives and policies around us.

 Authors' note

Discussions and actions that Chris has been involved in at CXK include:

- working to reduce, where possible, the number of miles staff drive by trying to place them in settings closer to home (not only does this help the environment, it also reduces the mental burden on the staff of having to drive further to work);
- actively working with the marketing team to print manual action plans on sustainably resourced paper;
- reducing the reliance on handouts when planning activities;
- not printing agendas for meetings.

The extent to which we can influence or affect change comes down to not only the will to do so, but also the cost and the willingness to sometimes make difficult decisions. For example, using action plans which are printed on sustainable paper can be more expensive than cheaper, less 'green' alternatives. Whiteboard pens that are reusable are more expensive to purchase in most instances than the regular pens.

Reflecting on the small things each of us can do to make a difference is at the heart of careers practice.

Depending on your viewpoint, you may (or may not) agree with the idea that lots of people making small changes can result in big impacts.

Reflecting on the environmental impact of writing this book and whether there was anything we could do to make it a greener process, we spoke with Trotman – who publish this book – who said that they organise lower but more frequent print runs of books to ensure they aren't left with excess stock, and their printers also use sustainable paper sources (which made us very happy).

The biggest impact (from a writing perspective) seems to be electricity. Our repective, domestic supplies aren't from reusable sources (neither of us yet have solar panels on our houses). However, we have both recently purchased electricity generators which run on solar power and come with their own solar array – powerful enough to charge a laptop and a mobile phone. Oddly, neither of us knew the other had done this until writing this section of the book!

It's a drop in the ocean . . . but a drop is still a drop and, in our opinion, small steps can lead to bigger ones.

Neither of us is in a position to shift to an electric car yet, but Chris plans to reduce his carbon footprint by cycling more and shifting from a large diesel van to a medium car, as well as using public transport where possible. He's also opted to return to using his electric motorbike more often, to reduce not only carbon emissions but also the noise and particle pollution a petrol motorbike produces.

Being 'greener' is a rabbit hole and it's not the purview of this book to weigh up the merits of one form of power over another, or to judge one approach over another. Rather, we aim to share ideas for consideration.

Some may argue that disconnection from all forms of technology is the way to be greener, whereas others may argue for mindful uses of technology as our salvation. For us, we argue that it is for each to be mindful and listen to their own reflections, taking responsibility for their own actions. We've chosen a middle way, whereas you may choose another (it's not for us to judge nor preach).

While you may, or may not, choose to work with an agenda of inspiring clients to aim for aspirational 'green' careers, we can all consider what we can do within our own lives and career practice to make the world a better place.

M

Magic

The late, great Terry Pratchett wrote about witches and wizards as characters who were dedicated to their craft.

They didn't always play well together – they liked their own company and didn't seek validation through others (or they liked to think so).

They valued information and wisdom, with each being unique, vibrant individuals. Some were in competition with each other; they debated and sometimes were at loggerheads (with different viewpoints or solutions to the issues they faced).

Most had a few good friends, or a network of peers, they leaned into for support . . . yet generally valued their solitude and time for quiet reflection or pragmatic calm.

However, when they were called upon, they would come together to change the world for the better.

We might all work for different organisations or have our own businesses. We might be in competition with each other (via our businesses). We might disagree about things and how things are done, but ultimately, we are all striving to make the world a better place for our clients.

We all care for, and look out for, each other on the whole (which is how we might be a bit different to Pratchett's witches and wizards). But we have much in common.

Many are eccentric, unique and beautiful characters, making this world a better place. Quietly offering guidance and pearls of wisdom to those who are lost or in need of support.

Isn't careers work, after all, a kind of magic?

Mistakes

'Mistakes' or 'failing' are actually the best way to learn.

A growth mindset embraces challenges and sees effort and resilience as a path to success. Setbacks are opportunities to learn and grow.

A fixed mindset assumes abilities are static and unchangeable – which we know from our prior learning experiences is untrue.

Have a growth mindset. Role model this with clients and colleagues. The aim of career development is not to be 'right'; it is to learn! For a bit more about growth mindset, go to the *Yet* part of this book.

 Authors' note

Chris was once working with a client in the early days of his career, when he was a Level 4 practitioner (early 2010s), and he had provided information in a session which, at the time, he thought was correct.

A few weeks later he was supporting another client interested in the same area and discovered that he had provided incorrect information in the previous session (he was mortified).

He went back to the office and shared this 'catastrophe' with his colleagues. A sensible and supportive colleague took him to one side and helped Chris realise no harm had been done. What was important was how he responded.

Chris contacted the previous client and sent the up-to-date information. The client messaged back, thankful and happy.

Chris learnt several things that day.

1. Mistakes sometimes happen and can be rectified.
2. You can't beat yourself up for what you didn't know at the time.
3. As career professionals, we will never know it all, as occupational information constantly changes and isn't always accurate in our sources. When we discover something new, we can add it to what we knew before.
4. It is always worth checking what we think we know and not to make assumptions.

Insider tips

You won't be everyone's cup of tea. Some people prefer Ribenna!

It's OK to make mistakes . . . learn from them when you do.

If it all goes wrong . . . tea and biscuits help, but returning to our Rogerian core conditions will resolve most things, in most situations.

Rogerian core conditions:

- Empathy;
- Congruence;
- Unconditional positive regard;
- Client-centred approach;
- Supportive environment;
- Facilitating growth;
- Focusing on the present.

N

No such thing as a silly question

Really, there is not!

Asking questions:

- is a fundamental tool for communication, learning and problem-solving;
- aids understanding;
- helps build engagement and develop relationships;
- shows genuine interest in others' perspectives;
- guides conversations;
- stimulates curiosity and critical thinking;
- helps us discover new ideas and solutions.

There are different types of questions which help us in our work.

Asking too many questions at once, and not allowing enough time to answer, can overwhelm the other person.

Instead, ask one question at a time and try not to speak over someone when they're replying. For longer or more introspective answers, allow them some extra thinking time, too.

And if you need them to elaborate, sometimes a brief pause is all it takes to prompt someone to expand on their answer.

There are various questioning techniques you can use to gain the information you need. Each technique has its own pros and cons.

- *Closed* questions are useful when you need a to-the-point answer, whereas *open* questions are good for extracting more detailed responses. Simple techniques such as *4 + 1 Questions* can be really helpful for reviewing progress and reframing.
- *Funnel* questions are a way to extract more detail gradually. This technique is a good way to prompt memories or deeper thinking.
- *Probing* questions help you gain detail and clarity. *5 Whys* is one example of ways to ask probing questions.
- *Leading* questions are a good technique if you're trying to persuade someone, but they can leave the other person feeling they have little or no choice.
- *Rhetorical* questions encourage reflection and are another useful persuasion technique.

Open and closed questions

A closed question usually receives a single word or very short, factual answer. For example, 'Are you thirsty?' The answer is 'Yes' or 'No'; 'Where do you live?' The answer is generally the name of your town or your address.

Open questions elicit longer answers. They usually begin with what, why and how. An open question asks the respondent for his or her knowledge, opinion or feelings. 'Tell me' and 'describe' can also be used in the same way as open questions. Here are some examples:

- What happened at the meeting?
- Why did he react that way?
- How was the party?
- Tell me what happened next.
- Describe the circumstances in more detail.

Open questions are good for:

- Developing an open conversation: 'What did you get up to on vacation?'
- Finding out more detail: 'What else do we need to do to make this a success?'
- Finding out the other person's opinion or issues: 'What do you think about those changes?'

Closed questions are good for:

- Testing your understanding, or the other person's: 'So, if I get this qualification, I will get a raise?'
- Concluding a discussion or making a decision: 'Now we know the facts, are we all agreed this is the right course of action?'
- Frame setting: 'Are you happy with the service from your bank?'

A misplaced closed question, on the other hand, can kill the conversation and lead to awkward silences, so is best avoided when a conversation is in full flow.

4 + 1 questions

1. What have we tried?
2. What have we learnt?
3. What are we pleased about?
4. What are we concerned about?
   +1 What do we need to do next?

What it does:

It can help people to think about a particular challenge or situation and plan for change. Because the 4 plus 1 questions are answered by more than one person, it groups together learning from different perspectives.

How it helps:

It can be used to update a one-page profile or to review a project or plan. It is a quick way to work out better ways of supporting people or working together.

Funnel questions

This technique involves starting with general questions and then drilling down to a more specific point in each. Usually, this will involve asking for more and more detail at each level.

Example:

'How many people were involved in the fight?' *'About ten.'* 'Were they kids or adults?' *'Mostly kids.'* 'What sort of ages were they?' *'About fourteen or fifteen.'* 'Were any of them wearing anything distinctive?' *'Yes, several of them had red baseball caps on.'* 'Can you remember if there was a logo on any of the caps?' *'Now you come to mention it, yes, I remember seeing a big letter N.'*

Using this technique, you can help someone to re-live an experience and to gradually focus on a useful detail. It is unlikely you would have got this information by simply asking an open question such as 'Are there any details you can give me about what you saw?'

When using funnel questioning, start with closed questions. As you progress through the tunnel, start using more open questions.

Funnel questions are good for:

- Finding out more detail about a specific point: 'Tell me more about Option Two.'
- Gaining the interest or increasing the confidence of the person you're speaking with: 'Have you used the IT Helpdesk?' 'Did it solve your problem?' 'What was the attitude of the person who took your call?'

Probing questions

Asking probing questions is another strategy for finding out more details. Sometimes it's as simple as asking your respondent for an example to help you understand a statement that they have made. At other times, you need additional information for clarification: 'When do you need this report by, and do you want to see a draft before I give you my final version?' Or to investigate whether there is proof for what has been said: 'How do you know that the new database can't be used by the sales force?'

- *Use questions that include the word 'exactly' to probe further: 'What exactly do you mean by difficult?' or 'Who, exactly, wanted you to do this?'*

Probing questions are good for:

- Gaining clarification to ensure that you have the whole story and that you understand it thoroughly.
- Drawing information out of people who are trying to avoid telling you something.

5 Whys
Getting to the root of a problem quickly

An effective way of probing is to use the 5 Whys method, which can help you quickly get to the root of a problem.

- The 5 Whys technique is most effective when the answers come from people who have hands-on experience of the process or problem in question.
- The method is remarkably simple: when a problem occurs, you drill down to its root cause by asking 'Why?' five times. Then, when a countermeasure becomes apparent, you follow it through to prevent the issue from recurring.

The 5 Whys uses 'countermeasures', rather than 'solutions'. A countermeasure is an action or set of actions that seeks to prevent the problem from arising again, while a solution may just seek to deal with the symptom. As such, countermeasures are more robust, and will more likely prevent the problem from recurring.

Have you ever had a problem that refused to go away? No matter what you did, sooner or later it would return, perhaps in another form.

Stubborn or recurrent problems are often symptoms of deeper issues. 'Quick fixes' may seem convenient, but they often solve only the surface issues and waste resources that could otherwise be used to tackle the real cause.

The method is remarkably simple: when a problem occurs, you drill down to its root cause by asking 'Why?' five times. Then, when a countermeasure becomes apparent, you follow it through to prevent the issue from recurring.

When to use a 5 Whys analysis:

You can use 5 Whys for troubleshooting, quality improvement and problem-solving, but it is most effective when used to resolve simple or moderately difficult problems.

You'll know that you've revealed the root cause of a problem when asking 'why' produces no more useful responses, and you can go no further.

It may not be suitable if you need to tackle a complex or critical problem. This is because 5 Whys can lead you to pursue a single track, or a limited number of tracks, of inquiry when, in fact, there could be multiple causes.

Leading questions
Leading questions try to lead the respondent to your way of thinking. They can do this in several ways:

- With an assumption – 'How late do you think your project report will be?' This assumes that the project will certainly not be completed on time.
- By adding a personal appeal to agree at the end – 'Lori's very efficient, don't you think?' or 'Option Two is better, isn't it?'
- Phrasing the question so that the 'easiest' response is 'yes' – our natural tendency to prefer to say 'yes' than 'no' plays an important part in the phrasing of questions: 'Shall we all approve Option Two?' is more likely to get a positive response than 'Do you want to approve Option Two or not?' A good way of doing this is to make it personal. For example, 'Would you like me to go ahead with Option Two?' rather than 'Shall I choose Option Two?'
- Giving people a choice between two options – both of which you would be happy with, rather than the choice of one option or not doing anything at all. Strictly speaking, the choice of 'neither' is still available when you ask 'Which would you prefer . . . A or B?' but most people will be caught up in deciding between your two preferences.

Note that leading questions tend to be closed.

Leading questions are good for:

- Getting the answer you want but leaving the other person feeling that they haven't got a choice.
- Closing a sale: 'If that answers all of your questions, shall we agree on a price?'

Use leading questions with care. If you use them in a self-serving way or one that harms the interests of the other person, then they can, quite rightly, be seen as manipulative and dishonest.

Socratic questions

Socratic questioning emphasises asking questions to stimulate thinking and exploration rather than providing direct answers or instruction.

The questions are open-ended, encouraging people to elaborate and think critically about a topic.

The aim is to challenge beliefs or assumptions, with the individual discovering answers and insights for themselves rather than being told what to think or believe.

The careers practitioner acts as a guide, helping the individual explore their own thoughts and ideas rather than directing them to a specific path or conclusion.

Examples of Socratic questions:

- What do you mean by that? (Clarification)
- How do you know that's true? (Evidence)
- What are some other possibilities? (Alternatives)
- What are the implications of that idea? (Consequences)
- What is the opposite of that? (Contrasting ideas)
- What assumptions are you making? (Underlying beliefs)
- How does this relate to what we talked about before? (Connecting ideas)

Rhetorical questions

Rhetorical questions aren't questions at all, in that they don't expect an answer. They're just statements phrased in question form: 'Isn't that creative?' 'I wonder how you produce such a fabulous finish on the wood?' 'How on earth can people work that machine so quickly?'

People use rhetorical questions because they are engaging for the listener rather than feeling that they are being 'told' something or expected to reply.

- Rhetorical questions are particularly useful when people are reluctant, or unable, to talk for example, if someone has Selective Mutism (a link to info about Selective Mutism can be found in the *Zone*).

Rhetorical questions are good for:

- Engaging the listener.
- Allowing people time to reduce anxiety about having to answer questions.

- Guidance is about being able to ask questions which help our clients reflect and find the solutions to their own situations. It is about being with our clients on their journey, not being the expert in the room pouring in solutions and knowledge from a jug.

- Our questions will be informed by our knowledge and we may impart information and advice when the situation calls for it. Yet the art of our practice is knowing when to hold back on offering up the information and advice. In knowing when a careful question to help a client consider their choices is more powerful than a waterfall of knowledge which may drown them.

- Don't forget to explain to clients why you are asking the questions you are asking (this will save a lot of confusion).

- Ask permission before exploring sensitive issues – with clients or other members of staff.

O

Opportunities

There are different models and theories which discuss the different stages of career planning and the opportunities these offer clients to explore their own career development.

Good reads

Try reading *Career Development Theories in Practice*, Julia Yates and *Career Development Theory Handbook*, Liane Hambly. And do check out the Career Marcr website. (You'll find the links to these in the *Zone*.)

Consider what the world looks like from your client's perspective – they are the ones who have to live with the decisions they are making and the life they are constructing.

To ensure we are truly capturing the client's thoughts, ideas and voice in our work, we can use a variety of methods to establish their perception of their opportunities.

Activities in a session which promote the development of self-awareness include:

- Mind clouds – where clients map out in clouds or bubbles what is important to them and/or the skills they have to navigate the future.
- Self-portraits – similar to the above but clients might create a portrait which shows how they feel about the future. This might be on paper as a drawing or using Lego to make a figure which shows how they feel. Having a range of different Lego faces in your toolkit can be helpful here. This can also be approached in a subtle way, as you could ask a client to make a model which represents themselves and where they

are at (from a selection of Lego). This can flag up any early concerns, especially where clients struggle to verbalise how they are feeling.

- Narrative – using props such as pictures, Lego or pipe cleaners to help clients tell a story or narrative which provides context for their current situation can be helpful.
- Blobs – a variation of the above, is that clients may take some Blu-Tack or modelling putty and make a blob which demonstrates how they are feeling. This might be a sphere which they smash or something stretched thin. It can be a very tactile way for clients to express themselves.
- Card sorts – card sorts outlining career management skills, identifying strengths or exploring opportunities are useful ways of helping clients to understand themselves. We've put some fantastic examples in the *Zone*!
- Posters – posters and worksheets are useful ways of helping clients understand different opportunities.
- Career mapping – where clients 'map out' with help from the career practitioner what is possible, is another way clients can discover what is out there and how they relate to each other. There are lots of different ways this can be done, from mapping out on paper or a smart screen to using opportunity cards for clients to work with. These are a highly tactile way of working and can be repositioned and moved around.
- Career as journey – clients may take a similar approach as the above but reflect on their current situation and the idea of a career as a journey. Particularly useful when clients get stuck and aren't considering all the paths to a particular job. This considers instead the career management skills they may need and the opportunities on the way to their goal which they may be able to take advantage of – adding value to their plan.
- Software – using careers software and digital tools can be incredibly helpful in identifying opportunities. Do use a trial version, or have it demonstrated to you, before purchasing, though. Different software suits different types of learners and learning.
- Not to be overlooked are the myriad websites that are out there which provide windows into various different sectors, from GoConstruct to Health Careers for the NHS. There are far too many to list!

Sometimes we are asked, 'how do you find these websites?'

The career websites of each home nation contain job profiles which have links to sector-specific websites and can be a useful place to start.

But often it is word of mouth from attending CPD events or via the careers community who share links online (such as via LinkedIn or Facebook).

Even if you never intend to post anything yourself, do use these online platforms which host careers communities as a way of picking up innovation and information.

- Careers quizzes – come in various shapes and sizes and can be useful for both self-discovery and awareness as well as opportunity awareness.

  It might be that you use a quiz in a session together or it becomes part of the career plan to take it home and complete, with the results being brought back to talk through.

  There are 'paid for' quizzes and career psychometric assessments which are available, but we are not intending to cover those in this book. It is also worth noting that quizzes and assessments don't work for all students; they can be useful as exploratory tools or jumping-off points for conversations for some.

  However, they are not a single 'go-to solution' on their own, as they often lack the required subjective nuance and can be open to misinterpretation.

- Physical and virtual tours – often found on establishment websites or YouTube channels. These are a great, easily accessible way for students and their families to explore and get a sense of a place. Using these in a career session can provide a talking point to reflect upon.

  Some industry sectors have been posting 'day in the life' videos on YouTube as well as other platforms such as Instagram and TikTok, providing students with useful insights.

  With each of these, being aware of bias is crucial, especially with videos looking to promote. Helping students to explore a mixture of different viewpoints develops their skills in researching and evaluating information. For example, videos shot and posted by an institution and separately by the students can help provide a nuanced balance and contrast well with each other.

- Insight videos – often shot by charities or sector bodies looking to support students. They can be really useful in 'filling the gaps' of information.

- Podcasts – there are numerous podcasts out there which can be helpful. When you find one that is great, do be sure to share your find with your colleagues.

- Open Public Lectures, MOOCs (Massive Open Online Courses are free online courses available for anyone to enrol) and UCAS Subject Tasters – attending open public lectures can be a really useful way to gain insights. Discussing how to find these (through a standard search engine) in a careers session can be useful for students.

- Books – from picture books through to traditional career books and insight guides, as well as biographies, to find out what various careers are like through the lens of lived experience. Books are amazing!

> You could work with your school/college librarian (if you have one) to build a library of not only career materials but also 'reading around the subject' starter guides.
>
> An initial reading list can be helpful for clients when provided alongside guidance about how they can follow their own intellectual curiosity.

- Work experience, work exploration activities and work shadowing – can be incredibly useful for providing insight. The new duty around KS3 work exploration focuses on providing students with a structured introduction to the world of work, including opportunities to explore different careers and gain valuable skills. This duty should be integrated into careers education programmes and can involve activities like career talks, work experience and exploring career pathways.
- Talking to friends and family – often overlooked, but helping students to explore who they have in their own network and who they could talk to can be incredibly worthwhile. If you find that they do not have this kind of network, you can help them develop a circle of support to help them with their career exploration ongoing.
- Lis McGuire RCDP has some useful activities to help clients identify possible sources of opportunity and people who can support with their careers research, using magnetic figures which connect together. Using similar tactile props such as these can be a great way for clients to explore who they have in their own networks that can help them, as well as identify who is in the network of people they know, whom they could access via them. You can find Lis on LinkedIn.

As careers practitioners, we end up learning a little about a lot rather than a lot about a little. A physicist can tell you all there is to know about string theory, whereas our knowledge needs to be just enough to show a client we understand where they are coming from.

P

Personalising action plans

We acknowledge that different practitioners will have varying approaches, and (depending on the organisation or contract area you work for) you may have some very specific guidelines you will be working within, which will affect not only what you write but also how much and for whom. It might be that you don't have the leeway to make your action plans more inclusive (by changing fonts and colours).

 Good read

In 2021, Liz Reece wrote a highly informative position paper for the CDI on action planning, which can be found in the *Zone*.

Chris contributed to this on behalf of CXK whose content is referenced within this.

For many of our clients with learning support needs, there is sometimes a tension between the action plan being a client-led process and a document written to support local authority transitions in a pre-16 and post-16 provision context, via the SEN and Learning Support systems in the UK.

To resolve this potential conflict of purpose, it is important for us to discuss the purpose of the action plan with our settings in advance of the work taking place.

We need to be mindful that some of the most client-centred ways of working won't always align with the formal requirements of some local authorities or the settings we find ourselves working in.

This doesn't mean that there needs to be conflict, as most of these issues can be resolved without drama and, most importantly, without placing the client-centredness of the sessions at risk.

Our approach to action planning just needs to be agreed upon before delivery to avoid misunderstandings around expectations.

There are a range of inclusive approaches to action plans which work for the clients we have been supporting. You can find out in more detail about inclusive tools and strategies in our previous book: *Career Development and Inclusive Practice*.

Where time is limited, we are aiming to work smarter where we can, rather than harder . . . especially while trying to maintain a work/life balance and look after our mental health.

However, with whatever approach we take to make this happen, ensuring clients remain at the heart of our choices is key.

For example, if we are using AI tools to support action planning and make efficiencies, we mustn't forget that good action planning requires our clients to be present and part of the process; we don't just cut and paste from a list of stock phrases or actions.

Clients are integral to the process.

 Insider tip

Don't write War and Peace for action plans. Clients don't need it and won't read it.

Philosophy and careers

We can't get away from who we are (the sum of our parts) – from our individual cultural influences, history and beliefs (philosophical or otherwise) through to the dominant narratives we tell ourselves and each other, which run through our lives.

Being aware of our individual perspectives and biases while we co-create meaning with our clients is vital to the work we do. Taking time to consider who we are and where we come from helps us to understand why we ask the questions we do.

Owning the reasons behind why we ask the questions we do (our agendas), and sharing the position(s) from which we practise with our clients, is crucial to an open approach and co-creation of meaning. Knowing why we are asking the questions we ask allows us to be transparent about our motivations and drivers, with our clients and ourselves.

Once a client is aware of our motivations, they can choose whether they wish to work with us or not. Through reflective practice, we can challenge ourselves, our agendas and sense of purpose to ensure we are being as open and as transparent as possible.

Exploring different philosophical positions which relate to the nature of work and career is something you could consider.

- What is the nature of truth and reality?
- How does this empower us in bringing different perspectives and ideas to our time with clients?

Philosophies for consideration:

As a starting point for a journey into philosophy, we've put together a list of some of the philosophical propositions we find interesting. It isn't a definitive list, as there are oodles of different philosophies out there. If you are curious to find out more, visit *Philosophy Corner* in the *Zone*.

- Ikigai – an approach which takes a pragmatic look at what we love, what the world needs, what we are good at and what we can each be paid for.
- Eudaimonia – often seen as the flip side of Hedonism, Eudaimonia emphasises the idea of seeking fulfilment through living virtuously and meaningfully according to our values. Know who you truly are + develop your unique potentials + use your unique potentials to fulfil your life goals.

- Hedonism – pleasure is paramount.
- Nietzsche considered pain as a catalyst for becoming stronger and overcoming difficulties, particularly if this was combined with purpose. *'He who has a why to live for can bear almost any how.'*
- Stoicism – seeking a life defined by justice, truth, self-control and courage.
- Confucianism – looks at the importance of virtues as a way to live a good life. However, it considers the importance of both the state and family, making reference to a specific moral code.
- Te Whare Tapa Whā – is a philosophy from New Zealand which integrates the importance of family and health into career theory.
- Socratic questioning – the pursuit of a line of questioning to get to a shared consensus or find meaning. Using open questions and exploring assumptions and bias by questioning what we consider to be true: 'What is good for our being?'
- Kaizen – a work-focused philosophy which is less about how to live; rather, instead, focused on how to work. The goal of kaizen is to make small changes over time to drive continuous improvement.
- Existentialism – either everything has meaning or nothing does! We could say that within an indifferent universe, life is what you make it (or make of it).

Western bias

For those of us practising in cultures based on Western tradition and thought processes, there is a danger of relying on Western philosophies alone. Exploring the great thinkers of the whole world is liberating and challenging, providing us and our clients with different ways to consider the world and what life might be, or mean, from many different perspectives.

Many philosophical positions also change and evolve over time and as they cross cultures – carried from one place to the next via trade, migration or social unrest and displacement.

We might find that philosophy helps us to consider what we each find meaningful or can make sense of in life. In turn, we can reflect on what we find senseless.

Chris' degree dissertation considered whether there can be a single fixed definition for art. He reasoned that there couldn't, as ultimately it was down to each individual, whether they found meaning or not in the art around them. In terms of art itself, and what made something art, it came down to the perception of the viewer and intention by the artist.

The same can be considered true of 'career' . . . and whether we can find sense in seeing what we do for work as a 'career' or not. Or even whether we can consider a 'career' as a thing in itself, which is a broader concept than 'work' alone.

Both of us use the term 'career' in a holistic way within our work – it encompasses all aspects of how we live our lives (including our hobbies and interests, as well as how we choose to live). Such a definition invites us to engage in discussion about the different ways we can live, and what that means for us at different times in our lives. It sees us moving beyond traditional conversations about work to explore lifestyle choices from ethical and philosophical viewpoints.

This helps us to consider, with our clients, their deeper motivations and sense of place in the world as they explore what is meaningful for them and why.

Our role can be in helping them to see themselves or discover, define, and find meaning in what it (career and/or life) is for them to be human within their unique and individual contexts.

Whether this is pursuing a lifestyle as a solarpunk or digital nomad, or building a life within a city as part of the 21st-century urban commuter class.

- Solarpunk is a literary, artistic and social movement that envisions and works towards actualising a sustainable future.
- A digital nomad is a person who works remotely while travelling and living in different locations, leveraging technology to stay connected and conduct their work.

So who's right?

Which philosophical position comes out on top?

For that, it will depend on what each of us is seeking . . . we will have to wait for further research if we are seeking an empirical answer! But do keep reading about philosophy in the meantime!

Working with each client where they are, with what they say they need, is crucial.

- The truth of each given situation is how that client is feeling (not our opinion of how we think they should feel). Due to this, delivering careers support with empathy and sensitivity is vital.
- Knowing our professional boundaries, and a personal library of agencies we can refer clients and their families to for further support, is useful.

We might find ourselves supporting clients whose purpose has been caring for family members. When that purpose has gone, they may find themselves adrift and without a sense of purpose or meaning. Helping them consider and discover what they find meaningful in who they are now (post-carer) can be a way to support them in challenging circumstances.

This may take time and they may be adrift for a while; they may not know how to help themselves, where to even start or when to be ready to start. Providing time and space, not leaping in to save them, but rather walk with them at the pace they need to go is important.

Exploring with them how much challenge they want from us, or different approaches we can take (coaching and/or guidance) is a useful way to establish boundaries around how we can support and be of service.

- How we each find purpose is reflected in how our clients respond in different ways to the world and their changing circumstances. From a practical viewpoint, asking clients whether they have (or can relate to) a motto or phrase they live their lives by (such as You Only Live Once) can be an illuminating way of helping them identify and explore what is important to them within their career planning and decision-making.

Most of us are a complex mixture of different philosophical positions . . . Some are viewpoints inherited from family members, and some are formed from our own reflections on the nature of existence or from engaging with social media, documentaries, reading and/or discussions with peers.

Many of us may change our views and decisions within different contexts or over time.

Perhaps such changeability in what we think, subscribe to and believe about life is in part what it means to be human. All of which affects our relationship to, and ideas about, 'career'.

It is also worth considering that many philosophies are not what they appear to be on the surface and deeper enquiries reveal hidden depths.

There are many different meaningful ways to live. We should reflect on where our own values and judgements land to reduce assumptions and unconscious bias, which may unduly drive or influence our approaches within careers work.

We will give the late, great, Douglas Adams (author of the *Hitchhiker's Guide to the Galaxy*) a final say on what meaningful is (spoiler alert!)

In his books, he provides the meaning of life as 42 – provided to us by the great supercomputer 'Deep Thought', whose purpose was to answer the ultimate question.

There is a fan theory that '42' wasn't just chosen as a random number. Douglas Adams was interested in computers when they were relatively new and shiny.

In ASCII code, the 42nd symbol is the Asterisk, which, in programming, is used as a wildcard (used to stand in for whatever you wish it to be).

- Therefore, if the meaning of life is 42 . . . life is whatever you wish it to be!

Beliefs and careers work

Philosophy sits alongside other beliefs which may influence what we do. Maybe something that gets shied away from in careers literature is the underpinning importance of personal belief systems in what we do. Whether Atheist, Agnostic, Buddhist, Christian, Emo, Hindu, Humanist, Klingon, Muslim, (or any other belief system) the nature of our own belief systems will play a part in our work.

Our beliefs and philosophical views are intrinsically part of us, shaped by so many things:

- upbringing;
- cultural heritage and race;
- the languages we speak;
- our circumstances growing up;
- finances;
- class and social status;
- sex and gender;
- disability;
- age.

All of these elements, and a whole load more, form a nuanced part of who we are, how we see ourselves and others, and how we construct meaning.

Our own individual circumstances, and the lens through which we see the world, are the only 'truth' we have.

So ask:

- How do we ensure we don't project our own beliefs onto others?
- How do we maintain a critical space of neutrality when a client's beliefs are different to our own?
- How do our beliefs help us get through the day?

Play

Why is this important?
Play:
- enhances cognitive skills, emotional regulation and physical coordination;
- promotes creativity and problem-solving;
- makes us resilient;
- helps us to build new neural pathways;

So, in modelling and engaging in play with our clients, we are helping them to develop their career-thinking brains.

Have fun!
There is an idea in some areas of UK work culture that 'work isn't meant to be fun' and that work is generally hard and difficult. Fun is seen to be for when you're not at work.

With echoes of the school playground, there is school time and playtime; time at work and home time.

Can work be play, or must it always be only a means to an end?

Do we live to work or work to live?

Or a mixture of both?

So much of our reality depends on mindset. Why can't we say that we have fun at work? If we alter our perception and give ourselves permission to have fun, to enjoy the moments when we are with our clients supporting them, it can be transformative for our day-to-day lives (and in turn our clients).

There will be moments that will be challenging and difficult, just as there are when we are not at work, but by being in the moment and having joyful purpose we can bring creativity and delight to our day-to-day work.

Q

Quick or slow

Pace yourself and your work
Things that help us to slow down:

- Have a cup of tea.
- Go outside and watch some insects.
- Take off our shoes.
- Engage with a bit of water – splash your face, run your hands under the tap, stand in the rain.
- Listen to something for a few minutes (music, a podcast, a stream, the wind).
- Breathe deeply.
- Play – with some Lego, a pipe cleaner . . . whatever takes your fancy.
- Consciously thinking about our pace and our audience.

Jules recently delivered a keynote speech at a conference in Europe where she was the only native English speaker. She received a super bit of feedback afterwards. Delegates said that they usually struggle to keep up with input delivered in English . . . often missing bits or not being clear on meaning. They fed back that they had not struggled with Jules' input.

Why? . . . Some of the things Jules did prior to delivering the keynote included:

- Sharing the slides with a colleague (from Estonia) to check for sense;
- Building in some gaps and pauses through movement – Jules checked with the organiser that she would be able to move around the room and still be heard;
- Pausing to explain some words;
- Immediately before the input, going outside for a few minutes.

And during the input:

- Having a hot coffee and a cold water nearby to touch;
- Thinking about slowing down and counting some pauses in her head;
- Using slides with pictures to create space and offer an alternative to words.

What helps you to slow down? Whatever it is, make sure you do it when your brain needs you to.

What do we do if there isn't enough time to see all our clients?

In some services and scenarios, there isn't enough time to see all our clients or spend the time we wish to with them. This can be deeply frustrating when we want to provide the best service we can.

There is no blame here. The shape of so many services is dependent on funding, whose models and purposes are different from each other and can sometimes change over time, as well as being limited.

There are situations within these scenarios which can be vexing, such as when a school doesn't purchase enough time from a careers provider to support their students, either due to a lack of funds or differing priorities, or where an individual has a dual role (e.g. Careers Lead + Career Development Professional) with not enough time to do either fully.

What can we do for our clients in such scenarios?

- As always, we do the best we can for them; part of this is not over-promising, as this can be just as frustrating for clients.
- Agree carefully with each client what realistically can be achieved in the time available.
- Signpost to other services and information.
- Be clear on the purpose of the service being offered to the client(s) even if we wish to offer more; staying within the remit of the service is key.

Ways in which we enable this can vary. Chris uses his Open Partnership Model (OPM). Part of the model focuses on the sharing of agendas/purpose and the position from which a practitioner approaches guidance.

This includes sharing the limitations of time, space and place at the start of a session. It also references referral and signposting to other forms of support and/or services as needed. We are part of a community of careers practitioners and supporters – what we cannot do within our own time constraints, someone else may be able to.

In many cases we are not the only person available who can help and support; nor should we be. The danger is that our egos can push us into believing that we are the only ones who can or should support.

This leads us to a slightly controversial position to consider.

Careers guidance doesn't work for everyone and isn't the solution for everyone

As passionate advocates for inclusive careers guidance, this may come as a surprise. Yet, being client-centred is to recognise that some clients don't gain value from careers guidance, struggle to engage with guidance, or don't like the idea of guidance.

Sometimes, clients don't like the idea of guidance at that time. Keeping the door open and not punishing clients for not wishing to engage is important, as we never know when they will need us.

This leans into Rogerian core conditions of Unconditional Positive Regard, Congruence and Empathy.

Authors' note

We have both worked with many clients over the years where this has been the case. Such as the student who shouted obscenities at Chris at the start of the academic year, where they said 'I'm not going to a @#$%&*! careers appointment!' then, in April of that same year, tracked him down and said 'I'm really stuck and need help . . . can I come and see you?'

And the young person at a college whom the staff informed Jules would not want to talk to her. Jules informed the college staff that she wanted to offer the young person an appointment regardless. The previous year, while still at school, this young person had not wanted to engage on the first two occasions Jules offered an appointment. On the third, they attended but did not speak much. On the fourth, they attended, engaged, and talked . . . eventually deciding to apply to the college.

Their response to being offered an appointment at college was a huge smile, and 'I thought you worked your magic on me last year . . . do I get to see you again!?'

Insider tips

As part of our ethics, we say that we won't judge.

We need to be true to ourselves and clients.

Congruence matters.

R

Realism

You will often hear people talking about what is 'realistic' for clients . . . particularly those who are not academic or have learning or physical support needs.

The laws across the UK say that adults (16+) are allowed to make unwise decisions . . . as long as they have the capacity to make the decision.

Have a think about what 'realistic' implies.

Maybe their career ideas are not realistic YET! They may develop career paths over time, and this then could become realistic for them – or sometimes tech solutions suddenly make the impossible possible.

We should only make best-interest decisions when a person <u>does not have the capacity</u> to make a choice.

And some people's 'unrealistic' ideas turn out to be inspired visions of their future selves!

Regardless of what turns out to be someone's realism, clients have the right:

- to impartial advice, guidance and information;
- to aspire and to dream;
- to a healthy and productive experience of exploring career ideas without judgement.

Principles of mental capacity, as stated by the Mental Capacity Act 2005 (England and Wales) and comparable legislation and guidance in many other countries:

1. Presumption of capacity:

Every adult is presumed to have the capacity to make their own decisions unless it is established that they lack capacity. Capacity means the ability to use and understand information to make a decision and communicate any decision made. A person lacks capacity if their mind is impaired or disturbed in some way, which means they're unable to make a decision at that time.

2. Supporting decision-making:

Efforts must be made to help and support a person to make their own decisions, and this should be done before assuming they lack capacity.

3. Unwise decisions:

A person is not to be treated as unable to make a decision merely because they make an unwise decision.

4. Best interests:

If a person lacks capacity, any actions or decisions made on their behalf must be in their best interests.

5. Least restrictive intervention:

Any actions or decisions taken on behalf of a person who lacks capacity must be the least restrictive of their basic rights and freedoms.

There are links to more information about mental capacity in the *Zone*.

Reflection

Reflective practice isn't just for passing our qualifications to become career development practitioners; it's a core part of who we are and how we practise.

Anything which affects the questions we may ask, or point of reference from which we practise, will affect the nature of our guidance.

Reflection helps us:

- tackle tricky ethical situations;
- consider our practice and ways we can improve;
- be kind to ourselves;
- challenge ourselves.

Here are a few things that might help you to reflect:

- Journaling.
- Drawing the day.
- Mind maps.
- Sticky note maps (which can be moved around to find patterns).
- Supervision with a trusted colleague or trained supervisor.
- Observe others delivering guidance.
- Get feedback from your peers.
- Collect client feedback on your practice (including action plans and resources you use). Do this regularly to help you improve.
- Learn from clients.
- Notice – reflect and check. Use all your senses. What do you see, feel, sense . . . Not just what you hear.
- Be observed! This is not always comfortable, but it is invaluable if you have an observer who will give you balanced feedback, ask questions and suggest alternatives.

Try different techniques and strategies and, however you reflect, do it on a regular basis. Reflect on outcomes as well as actions.

Do your best to make it accurate to avoid the often referenced 'hall of mirrors' which distorts our reflections on what has happened.

 **Insider tips**

Be mindful of when your own personal beliefs make impartiality challenging.

Recognise when you aren't the right person to help.

Celebrate impact to the same extent as you identify areas for development.

Learn from your own experience and from others.

We have put a link to the **CXK** reflective practice tool in the *Zone*.

Refreshments

Workplace culture is a funny old thing to crack. As a CDP, you will probably find yourself working across a wide range of different settings. Within each, you will find a variation in culture and expectations. Often, there are unspoken rules which can be confusing.

- In some places, there is an unwritten rule that you should 'contribute' and bring in a packet of biscuits or cake every so often, for the rest of the staff to enjoy, even if you are a guest or visitor.
- If it's your birthday and you are at work, some places expect you to bring in cake to share.
- In some places, there is a petty cash tin and staff are expected to pop in a pound coin every so often, so there is enough money for milk for tea or coffee. Even if you are a visitor.
- There may be communal coffee available [which is rather cheap and tastes like mud] and lots of people's own 'nice' tea or coffee in the staff room as well.

 Insider tips

When you start in a new setting, ask what the expectations are about things like bringing stuff in, paying, using other people's mugs or coffee, using the fridge.

Exercise caution in the staff kitchen!

If you aren't there all the time, you might not be able to learn or pick up what the unwritten rules are.

Chris and Jules are incredibly lucky – with colleagues keeping them supplied with 'nice coffee' and biscuits! #winning

So how do you get to such a position?

Answer – 'be good at your job!'

- attend to relationships with all staff across the setting;
- go the extra mile;
- demonstrate, through actions and outcomes, what independent careers guidance can do for clients.

Be aware that in some settings they assume you will bring in your own travel mug with safety lid for hot tea or coffee (some won't allow the use of regular mugs in case hot tea or coffee is spilt on a client).

Without your cup, you arrive before the sessions start (to set up), you go to make a coffee and are left with nothing to drink at the start of the day . . . not the best start for those of us who need our caffeine to get rolling! Although this is a slightly whimsical example, being mindful of our own needs is crucially important. In the rush to meet the needs of our clients, we sometimes overlook our own. This can include our mental health needs and being aware of what we need to find and maintain balance.

This is especially true if we are in the middle of the day, in between client sessions, and perhaps dealt with a particularly tricky situation. This could be something like a safeguarding issue, or a session which was clunky or mentally draining.

There is nothing wrong with saying that you need to delay your next session by five minutes so you can have a breather. Whether to just sit and catch your thoughts or even take yourself outside, to literally get some fresh air. You are no good to your next client if your mind is still reeling due to the previous session.

Being mindful of our personal headspace and whether we are thirsty or hungry is really important. Schedule in breaks and ensure you take your lunch . . . it's amazing how easy it is to forget to look after ourselves and in doing so, not be in the headspace to support our clients.

If you know you need a few minutes in between each appointment, structure your day to enable this. You could offer to collect each client from reception, or a classroom, giving you the opportunity to move around between appointments; and to take the scenic route if you need some fresh air or a quick snack.

'In my early days as a Careers Adviser I wondered why a client couldn't focus . . . I realised halfway through, they were fixated on my lunchbox as they hadn't had breakfast and were hungry. I kicked myself afterwards and now do my best to be mindful of this.' Chris T

 Insider tip

When setting up your room for career sessions . . . don't leave your lunchbox out.

Lunch

In our hectic day-to-day work it is easy to keep pushing on with admin or supporting clients and not look after ourselves. Making sure to take lunch is important.

Taking a lunch break provides a vital opportunity to reset and recharge. Stepping away from your chair allows your brain to shift focus, reducing cognitive fatigue. This can significantly lower stress levels and help prevent burnout.

Try engaging in a relaxing activity during your break – drawing, going for a walk or enjoying a meal mindfully can help boost your mood.

Getting out into natural light and fresh air increases serotonin levels, helping to reduce feelings of anxiety.

S

Sick and tired

Is a change as good as a rest? What to consider if you are struggling, or bored, in your current role:

- Having a careers session with a trained practitioner who works with adults.
- Changing to another part of the sector.

> - ✔ The *Careers in Careers* guide by Caroline Green and John Paley may help you to consider where else you may wish to pivot to and the diverse range of roles available in the sector.
> - Taking a break and doing something completely different for a while.

For all of us, anxiety can become a feature in our lives.

Recognising and being aware of the pressures on our clients is vital.

Today might not be the day to make a decision or even the right day for a careers conversation.

It might be the day to take a pause, get off the metaphorical treadmill.

Maybe it is the day to just be with them, so they know that the careers space is a safe space.

If it is the day to start exploration, it might not be exploration of hopes and dreams, career pathways or goals. It might just be the day to explore who they have in their corners; the wider support networks available to them.

Consider:

- Who are their champions?
- Do they know what support services are available to them?
- Are they accessing support?
- If not, is there a specific reason why they feel that they can't or don't wish to access support?

People should never be pressured into support, especially around mental health. It is something which should be considered by the individual and pursued when they are ready.

How will I know you're not OK?

It is important that we look out for ourselves and each other.

Make sure your supervisor and/or your colleagues know how to tell when you are not OK.

You can have this as a standard question when you start supervision with someone new.

'How will I know you're not OK?' is best discussed when you are OK. If you don't know for yourself, ask people close to you how they can tell when you are not OK. It is incredibly useful for a colleague or manager to be able to spot the signs and let you know you are exhibiting them . . . often other people notice before we do!

Some organisations also have dedicated emotional wellbeing services for staff to access, including access to occupational health and healthcare. Check to see what your health plan covers.

 Insider tip
Breaks are not a luxury – they are necessary for maintaining a healthy mind.

Studies show that taking regular breaks actually enhances productivity. Continuous work without breaks is counterproductive as fatigue sets in. Your lunch break acts as a brain refresher, allowing you to return to your work with renewed energy and focus.

Our job is also often quite sedentary – we sit for extended periods during interviews and at our desks.

This has implications for physical health. Incorporating movement into your breaks, even if it's just a short walk, can mitigate some of these risks. It improves circulation, promotes better posture and helps reduce stress.

Build a habit of taking breaks from the start. It sets a precedent for prioritising self-care and boundaries.

Social media

Social media and technology ... for business

Technology is ubiquitous in the modern world and none more so than the internet and with it the rise of social media. Without taking a deep dive into the many platforms and their uses, as well as the ethics of social media, it does have a place in practice in various forms.

It is a useful tool for the business functions of what we do, enabling us to reach out to not just clients but also customers and wider society.

- For the sake of coherency, it is worth noting that in this book we define those we directly work with (providing personal guidance to) as our clients (e.g. students in schools and colleges) and those we form business contracts with as our customers (e.g. the headteachers or senior leadership in schools and colleges). We are aware that within some services, 'customers' refers to 'clients'.

Social media use ... for clients

Guardrails and caution are worth exercising. A careful use of social media and using SEO (Search Engine Optimisation) can benefit most businesses, whether you are self-employed or work for large organisations.

It can also help us with our own practice and relationships with our customers. Chris has had a number of follow-on conversations with different schools, following posting client case studies on LinkedIn where one school has seen what has happened in another and asked for similar in their own setting. This has included everything from assembly topics through to ways of organising and structuring career sessions.

The flipside of social media is the ease with which it is possible to have what would normally be a private conversation in a public space.

- Words can be misconstrued and come back to haunt us later.
- Seemingly well-intentioned posts can spiral out of control and create reputational damage.

As much as many of us like to have the last word, it doesn't mean we should or ought to. Sometimes the best thing to do is walk away from the computer or phone and not say anything.

These are our top tips for dealing with social media:

- If in doubt, don't post or comment.
- Don't get drawn into arguments.
- Never post or comment if overly tired, emotional, angry or worn out.

- If unsure if your post is worthy/meaningful, sleep on it and decide the next day.
- If unsure if your post is saying what you want it to, ask a friend, family member or colleague to sense-check it.
- Be polite.
- Avoid inflammatory language.
- Never revert to personal insults or slurs about people or organisations (no matter how you might feel).
- If it is a public conversation, and a private conversation may be more appropriate, DM (Direct Message) the person you wish to speak to.
- Be prepared to agree to disagree – you don't have to persuade everyone to agree with your world view.
- Unasked-for advice is often unwanted advice – don't offer advice if the context doesn't ask for it.
- Remember everyone has feelings... be respectful and exercise empathy.

Many employers have policies regarding social media misuse, such as a bar on posting or making any comments that may bring an employer into disrepute. In many cases, this can result in disciplinary action even if comments were made on a non-business to business platform and/or via a personal account.

Knowing when to not say anything (keeping our mouths shut) and when to challenge can be one of the hardest things to discern.

So how do we know when to act or not?

We would like to say we have always known when and when not to say things, and that years of experience have honed our judgement... sadly this isn't always the case for even the most experienced of us!

What we try to do now is consider whether it is ethical and refer back to not only our Code of Ethics but also our own value bases.

If you believe that not saying anything would harm clients, try to step up and write a respectful reply on posts.

An example would be an education professional saying something that was factually incorrect and knowing they were actively sharing this information with clients.

Social media and technology... with clients
Using social media with and/or for clients is an interesting one. We can find ourselves using technology across multiple devices and in different ways... from 'Ed-Tech' as an all-encompassing panacea, being championed by some

and reviled by others, through to the rapidly emerging use of AI (Artificial Intelligence) and explorations of how it can be used to provide more efficient ways of working.

These gifts or curses are occurring within our careers sphere; let's get into it . . .

Careers commentator and influencer Jake Richings has posted on this topic with great clarity, challenging us as practitioners to make the most of social media and new technologies to support our clients.

He has given Chris pause to think about what he creates for CXK in the way of content to be shared on various social media platforms, as well as confidence to be bolder in his vlogs which, alongside more traditional blogs, he writes for clients, parents and carers.

Chris started making vlogs for CXK during the Covid-19 pandemic, as access to schools and students was reduced. He was motivated to create content to support clients attempting to make decisions within complex times . . . it definitely wasn't to be noticed or to be an influencer of any sort!

Social media created a means to disseminate the vlogs and blogs, to reach a wider audience.

During this time, Chris felt that even if one client watched one of his vlogs and it helped them, it was worth doing.

Looking back, Chris feels these very early vlogs are 'cringe', but everyone has to start somewhere and with practice, his vlogs have improved and continue to form part of CXK's YouTube channel and the freely accessible CXK Careers Hub.

There are myriad different ways social media can be used as a platform:

- to bring in employers to settings, via virtual or live-streamed tours;
- for discussions or presentations;
- to link remote places and people to larger places with more opportunities or to show alternative possibilities. The most extreme example of this has probably been the times that the international space station astronauts have given talks to school children or when the rovers on Mars have sent back images and videos (you can't get much further away than that!).

It also allows those who struggle to communicate within traditional settings an equitable environment to interact with others.

Perhaps a space for career guidance sessions within virtual reality (VR) environments will be possible soon, harnessing the creativity of untapped possibilities in such spaces.

> Social media as a platform for career sessions themselves, is still an untapped and potentially underexplored resource in many settings due to the complexity of GDPR and data protection legislation.

From an ethical viewpoint, we know that it isn't appropriate to have private conversations in public spaces (whether these are in physical or virtual spaces), but the DM functions and chat rooms of social media allow us to take public discussions into private environments. However, the protections to keep clients and practitioners safe are reduced unless safeguards are built in.

Career organisations and self-employed practitioners that use direct messaging and social media with clients need safeguards, processes and monitoring to maintain safety, to protect themselves and their clients. Most will have DPOs (Data Protection Officers) and MIS (Management Information System) managers to keep staff and clients safe; those that don't employ any directly have access to consultants for advice.

Data protection and security are just as important as child protection, especially in a more information-heavy age. Fines and consequences for breaking legislation can be severe, with ignorance being no defence.

 Insider tips
Use your GDPR training as an opportunity to reflect.

Social media use . . . for CPD
Technology is useful not just for networking but also for our own development. There are CDI and Career Leaders groups on Facebook as well as numerous development groups on LinkedIn.

Several newsletters and key proponents are worth following on LinkedIn, posting regularly on career matters within the careers sphere. There are far too many to make an exhaustive list here but there is a mixture of practitioners, writers and academics out there (so if there is something you are looking into, there is probably someone writing about it!).

Our personal list includes . . . Bella Dowsell, Caroline Green, Chris Oliver, Chris Webb, Ciara Bomford, Dierdre Hughes, Janet Colledge, John Ambrose, John Paley, Katherine Jennick, Liane Hambly, Lis McGuire, Lorna Stalker, Lucy Satler. There are many, many more – but if you start with some of these, they will open you up to a great selection of voices across the profession.

Social media is useful for establishing relationships with like-minded souls in the careers sphere who can support us, as well as networking with employers and different sectors to explore and research what is involved within various occupations.

It can, however, feel somewhat overwhelming! So how can we make sense of it all?

How do we stay on top of everything? The straightforward answer is . . . we don't!

There isn't enough time to read everything that is out there, even if you spent all of your working and free time doing so.

What is needed is a strategy that works for you.

- Base the focus of your CPD on your practice.
- Reflect on what you are struggling with in your day-to-day practice (whether occupational knowledge, approaches or models and theories) and apply this to your CPD.
- Look at your client base and undertake CPD based on this.
- Don't try and read everything.

By all means keep a cursory look at the wider sector and developments, but don't try to keep up with everything. You will burn out if you do!

Staying safe

If you are not safe, you can't be impartial.

Do not 'do nothing' if someone is unsafe.

You should be told on arrival about:

- signing-in arrangements;
- safeguarding policies and procedures;
- where the fire assembly point is;
- where the toilets, staff room and tea/coffee facilities are.

If you are not told – ask.

Make sure your safeguarding training is current. Safeguarding is central to everything that we do – it protects vulnerable individuals from harm, abuse, and neglect, ensuring their wellbeing and promoting their rights.

This involves creating a safe environment, preventing potential risks and responding effectively to any instances of harm.

All people working in a position of trust with children and vulnerable adults require safeguarding training.

Organisations working with vulnerable groups should have robust safeguarding policies and procedures in place and ensure staff receive appropriate training. This should happen, initially, before you do any direct work with clients.

If you are working freelance, you can source training through local authorities or organisations who focus on the welfare of vulnerable people – we've put links to some examples in the *Zone*.

- Do check that your training adequately covers the role you will be in. Some training is specific to children or to adults. If you are working with anyone 18+, you should do both. The legislation for safeguarding children and safeguarding vulnerable adults is quite different.
- Safety always comes first.

Some of our settings are higher risk than others due to their location or the cohort of clients – for example, if you are in a setting which is not staffed while you are there, working in someone's home or with clients who have previously presented a risk to themselves or others.

If you are working in a higher-risk setting, there are some simple things you can do to reduce risk generally:

- tie your hair up;
- no jewellery;
- no sharp objects;
- work in a room with a window where people can see you, or leave the door open;
- stay calm (use breathing and grounding techniques as a habit, not just in response to a situation arising);
- ensure you have radios (walkie-talkies) and/or access to a phone;
- sit near the exit in the room.

This does not replace doing a specific risk assessment for your particular situation and environment. A good place to start finding out more about risk and personal safety is *The Suzy Lamplugh Trust*. And ask your employer for some training.

Before you start working in any setting, find out if someone has done a risk assessment. If not, do one.

Risk assess – reduce risk where possible – leave if necessary.

 Authors' note

A probation client came to see Jules and was visibly very agitated. Clients were sent as part of their probation order, so they felt obliged to attend! Jules did not feel safe.

Jules: 'You seem upset, we can leave this for another time – I'll tell your PO we've rearranged. I'll let you go now.'

Client: 'I'm going to leave now.'

Client the following week: Apology . . . thanks . . . engagement.

Jules took the exit option here to allow time and space. Both people were safe. The engagement in subsequent appointments was superb.

The same applies to colleagues if they verbalise that they are going to put themselves in an unsafe situation . . . take action, tell a manager or safeguarding lead.

We have a motivation to help people which sometimes leads to us overlook the risk to ourselves.

Staying Safe

 Authors' note

Two colleagues were discussing how one of them could approach the following situation: a home visit request from a client with known offences against women. They were discussing the risk assessment. This involved things like — park round the corner to avoid the client seeing the car registration, a phone call on arrival and exit. Another colleague told Jules as they were concerned. Outcome — no home visit. Another colleague present in the building. Door open.

 Insider tips

Stick to your boundaries . . . it will keep you safe.

You may be asked for your DBS or Disclosure Scotland certificate before you begin working with clients 1:1, so take it with you when you first visit a setting or client. There is more information about the different kinds and levels of checks in the *Disclosure and Barring* section.

T

Transitions

This is an often-overlooked aspect of the DOTS model:

- Decisions;
- Opportunities;
- Transitions;
- Self.

Transitions involve moving from a known and comfortable state to an unknown and uncertain one, often triggering feelings of fear, anxiety and potential loss.

When we talk to clients about moving on in their career path, we are asking that people let go of the familiar, adapt to new roles, relationships and environments and leave what they know behind.

Even positive transitions hold uncertainty and the need to adjust to a new way of being.

Using techniques which support our clients to 'move' helps enable effective transitions.

- Co-production of plans is far more meaningful than being 'told'.
- Rest before planning transition activities is helpful – does it need to take place in a separate session?
- Does the client need a movement break?
- Are they overwhelmed?
- Do they need time to process what has been explored so far?
- Do they have sufficient headspace to plan alone – or do they require a circle of support to help them?

- Has a process been established which links the career session and action planning into the wider transition process (this could be with a SENCO, parents/carers or the client's wider support network)?
- How much is too much? Your client may only need one or two actions as part of their next steps. What is the right amount at this stage for them?
- Will you be able to see them again? If not, is there a way to 'handover' support for transition activities and follow up to another supporter whom the client trusts?

Some parents of students may also have their own support needs and find the complexity of the education and training system too much of a challenge to navigate adequately, thus requiring greater advocacy for them and the clients you are working with. Understanding where and how you can tap into greater support for parents, as well as your immediate client, is important as one affects the other. This might be via specialist local authority services, social services, community and voluntary sector or via their education setting.

Discussing strategies which have worked with clients in the past is a useful way to start. However, this is not a guarantee that they will work for them now as they plan their career transitions.

Careers coach and writer Polly Wiggins raises some important insights about transitions:

> *for some (former carers) there may be quite a long transition period when it comes to reassessing their purpose. This can also be true of people who have recently become ill or been diagnosed (moved from 'able' to 'disabled') – this is a transition period that might go on for some time. People in this transient state may genuinely not know what has meaning for them anymore, which means the role of the careers practitioner might be in supporting them towards finding out. This transition may be a time of chaos and confusion and can be deeply painful and challenging to negotiate. Empathy, patience, respect and kindness are absolutely vital here. We must not try to hurry people.*
>
> *People with illnesses/disabilities may also have complex feelings about them, their lives, and their careers. I genuinely believe my experience of disability has taught me useful things, but I also simultaneously feel very sad about it. I both wish for a different life and also wouldn't change a thing. Cognitive dissonance is common!*

U

Unconditional positive regard

Unconditional positive regard means accepting and respecting others as they are without judgement or evaluation!

This sounds easy – we are all supposed to be 'impartial' after all. However, we are all human and sometimes our personal views, emotional responses and preferences affect our work.

Don't ignore these uncomfortable feelings when you have them – that's when to utilise supervision or phone a friend. Reflect on why you are struggling to hold positive regard and discuss strategies to address the unhelpful feelings so that they don't get in the way of effective delivery.

Unconscious bias – where we make judgements or decisions on the basis of prior experience, our own personal thought patterns or assumptions, and we are not aware that we are doing it – is always something to keep an eye out for. Having a trusted colleague to help you check your own biases is really useful.

Dangers of comparison
We can get caught in the comparison trap, comparing the needs of one client to another. The risk becomes that we start to judge the 'need' of each and how we think they should be handling things.

> **Authors' note**
>
> Chris can remember working with a client who was facing multiple barriers: low grades, parents divorcing, illness and potential homelessness. This client was pragmatic but remained, despite the odds, focused on building a future for themselves. Another client Chris saw that day was one who was worried they were going to get Cs rather than Bs in their GCSEs (note this was before the changes to numbers for GCSE grades).
>
> A teacher supporting the career sessions remarked, 'I don't know what they have to complain about; it's not like they're facing the same issues as the other child!'
>
> This rattled Chris, as he could see that both students were facing barriers and worries which needed support. From their individual perspectives, each was facing issues which were important to them.
>
> The truth, however, is unique to each client and indeed ourselves. Life is not only what we make it but how we perceive it. Both clients needed support; just because one was seemingly coping better than the other, or because one's needs were more complex than another's, it didn't mean that one client needed guidance more than another.

Specific circumstances of clients will affect us all in different ways. Here are a couple of examples from our own experience.

Short lives

Working with a young person with a life-limiting condition or life-threatening illness can be emotionally overwhelming at times, and it is important that you get the emotional support you need.

It is important to be able to reflect on your own emotional state.

Make sure you have the support you need – through supervision, peer support or counselling.

And if you're ever really struggling and don't have that support, reach out. If we can't help you, we probably know someone who can!

> **Authors' note**
>
> Jules' experience (many years ago) of being told by a manager – after the deaths of six clients in six months – that she 'should be used to it by now' was not only unhelpful but seriously impacted her ability to work.
>
> It wasn't a totally bad experience (we always learn the most powerful lessons through things not working), but at the time, it felt desperate.
>
> The six young people who died were all, without exception, a joy to work with. Some of the outcomes before their deaths were extraordinary given the circumstances. So, it is a situation well worth the challenge and the emotional impact – but you do not need to do it alone. We are a careers community, and we can be there for each other when we experience loss.

The careers community is a supportive and helpful space. Do not struggle alone. It doesn't help you or the client. To offer the support and guidance we are there for, we need to also be our best selves.

- Ask for support.
- Give support to others.
- Acknowledge that we are all human beings and emotionally impacted by the people we work with and for.

There is a great organisation called *Together for Short Lives* who offer information and advice to families. They have information on transition, bereavement support, end-of-life planning and a summary of professional and family publications – links are in the *Zone*.

Offenders

Career guidance can significantly reduce reoffending by ensuring that people develop the skills and confidence to enable them to lead purposeful lives within their communities.

Working with this client group can be hugely rewarding.

Authors' note

It was this area of work that motivated Jules to train as a careers adviser initially. Investigating a range of potential careers, she volunteered with the probation service. Working with one young man who was excluded from school, and at the time illiterate, she learnt from his perspective what exclusion does to people.

Together they took small steps, spent time learning to trust one another, to be honest, to challenge one another. He swallowed his pride and let Jules teach him to read and write. They went together to see the headteacher at his old school – did a persuasive double act and got him back into school. He went on from there to do an apprenticeship – earning, learning and flourishing.

Jules found a passion she could turn into a career and has always enjoyed working with clients facing challenges to inclusion.

There have been times when Jules has not felt very comfortable working with particular clients due to the nature of their offences.

After spending a year working with sex offenders, Jules felt she was struggling to remain impartial and that the work was affecting her mental wellbeing. She reflected on this with her manager, and they both agreed it was not appropriate for Jules to continue working with this particular cohort.

The Career Development Institute's Code of Ethics holds members to account professionally:

Re. Impartiality – our code asks that:

Members will maintain awareness of any limitations on their impartiality, acknowledge potential impact and take a neutral and non-directive approach when working with clients. Where impartiality is not possible, members will declare this to the client promptly.

And regarding fitness to practise:

Members will embrace reflective practice and maintain their fitness to practise in terms of their personal integrity, physical and mental wellbeing.

Insider tip

If you are struggling to hold unconditional positive regard . . . talk to someone about it!

V

Visibility

Be seen!

Wherever you are working, make sure people know who you are and why you're there.

Why?

- It raises the profile of our profession.
- It helps keep you safe.
- The more people who engage with you, the better your odds of finding someone really useful.
- If people talk about you knowledgeably with others, this will help to alleviate anxiety in clients who may be unsure about meeting with you.

W

What should I wear?

From tattoos to nose rings, bright red hair to unconventional attire, feeling like yourself and professional dress . . . For many years, the debate with regards to dress codes and 'being professional' seems to have gone hand in hand.

When Chris first started in careers, the expectation around dress was loosely referred to as 'social work-esque'. Men were expected to wear a shirt, tie, a smart jumper and trousers in educational settings. Smart enough to be smart but not so casual as to be too casual. In the mid-00s, the emphasis shifted to what was referred to as 'business dress' which meant wearing a suit and tie.

When Jules first started, she received a complaint from the office manager for wearing trousers to work!

As we enter the mid-20s of the 21st century, Jules and I have found the dress codes in educational establishments to be highly pluralistic. In one school, a shirt and tie or suit is an expectation, while in another, a t-shirt or polo neck is acceptable. Thankfully – due to increasing temperatures – many schools have relaxed their summer dress code to include wearing shorts.

Contact the setting you are going to before you go in to deliver and ask them if they have any expectations! If your style of dress will not be meeting expectations give them a quick explainer – for example, I will be wearing a baseball cap because I'm photosensitive and won't be able to function properly without it.

Clothes and 'professionalism' are more complicated than they may first appear, for our clients and us; they are signifiers, leading to concepts of identity and power when we look at them from the viewpoint of semiotics.

What Should I Wear?

> Semiotics is the study of signs and symbols and how they create meaning. We use language, gestures and other systems – including adorning our bodies – to communicate. These systems shape our understanding of each other and the world. Semiotics explores the intentional, and unintentional, ways that signs convey meaning, including visual, linguistic and cultural elements.

Understanding and taking ownership of this is useful.

> **Authors' note**
>
> Chris can remember some of the snobbery within the careers community when he first started as a careers practitioner, being cautioned about 'looking too much like a youth worker'.
>
> The last thing he wanted to do was to dress too casually, as this may signal that he wasn't a 'professional'. He found this uncomfortable on several levels: a lack of nuance around understanding context, as well as congruence and identity.
>
> Youth workers are professionals who have approaches grounded in theory and understanding. To be dismissed as looking 'merely like a youth worker' was to disregard the rigour of this fellow profession.

Context matters.

Turning up to a community centre to engage with young people who are disengaged from education in a full suit and tie is often inappropriate. It can signal a power imbalance and put up a barrier.

However, to turn up very casually attired in a private school, where the dress code is formal, could signal a lack of understanding of etiquette, discipline and expectations, as well as (regardless of whether we agree or not) how some people will judge us and our abilities based on our dress.

So, consider other people's perspectives before making your choice. You can still make your own choice . . . but it is good to reflect on what we might be signalling.

And do consider if you have too much flesh on show – this can be very distracting for others!

Taking a deeper dive into identity, using Carl Rogers' core conditions, a key aspect of this is congruence and being ourselves. To dress as 'someone else' is to break with this congruence.

Some argue that dressing to 'play a part' can do wonders for confidence, as you dress to fill a role. It becomes like armour. There is merit to this and if it works for you, then go for it.

 Authors' note

Chris found that he struggled to be himself in the early days of careers work. At the time, he didn't know he was neurodivergent and had come from an art school culture which was a lot more relaxed and informal. As a former personal tutor and art teacher he could dye his hair red and wear a nose ring within that context, yet within the careers sphere in Kent at the time, this was very much frowned upon for men.

In a shirt, tie and later a suit, Chris struggled to be himself (although he was able to wear his trilby hat as a small nod to being 'unconventional').

While training to become a CDP, he attempted to deliver careers guidance as his mentors would (whom he admired); yet inside he struggled with Imposter Syndrome, identity and feeling like a fraud.

This was before he was 'fully sleeved' with tattoos covering both of his arms.

As an ADHDer wearing a suit and trying to deliver like others was, looking back, an ultimate form of masking to conform to societal expectations.

It nearly broke Chris, emotionally and mentally.

As an art student, Chris, like many others, had played with identity and clothes . . . from punk to ska-derived fashion choices (even a dalliance with goth culture!). Earlier, while at secondary school as a student, he had struggled to fit in and be himself, yet when he became an art student and later an art teacher, he was able to unmask to a greater extent and be himself in a place which was a better fit (although not completely, as he struggled with some of the behind-the-scenes aspects of being a teacher in Further Education).

To be suddenly working within a 'business dress' culture at the age of twenty-eight, within careers, was a shock to the system for Chris.

As we grow into ourselves, the choices we make about what we wear signal who we are to others, as well as to ourselves (there is a wealth of literature which can be explored on this topic). Being as comfortable as we can within our own skin, understanding ourselves and our unconscious biases, before we help others, is an important aspect of development as a Careers Professional.

How did Chris adapt and survive (and eventually thrive)?

The continual masking was getting to Chris, as he struggled to balance his inner and outer worlds. About six years into his 'career in careers', the funding changes coincided with Chris seizing control of his identity. In one way the funding changes were liberating, as convention gave way to organised chaos, and no one knew how things would land in the long term for the careers sector.

Over the next few years, several things happened for Chris which coincided with identity, careers practice and his sense and understanding of 'professionalism'.

He was in his mid-30s and finally understood that 'being himself' is to be congruent and in doing so, offer a better 'professional service' which was still grounded in models and theory; informing his practice.

This led him to become playful once more with his identity and choosing clothes which were 'him' . . . from waistcoats to pocket watches.

He also made the decision to become fully sleeved with his tattoos.

This wasn't without consequence, and Chris thought long and hard before deciding. A potential consequence would be to live a life where wearing long-sleeved shirts (even in summer) might be the requirement due to dress codes in some settings.

The choice to be fully tattooed has had a myriad of effects on his practice . . . some unexpected, others less so.

From students who are part of the 'alternative scene' more readily relating to him, to being a role model for those with ADHD and others who don't necessarily easily fit within some settings, this shows that you can be your unique self, be expressive, have ADHD and still be professional.

Chris has had numerous occasions where students have gone . . . 'You have ADHD' or 'You have tattoos, but you have a job . . . I can too'.

Yet Chris is far from unique in seeking to express his individuality and sense of self. The changing attitudes towards tattoos and similar traditional alternative cultures within the workplace are an interesting phenomenon to observe.

A search online of 'corporate goth' reveals a plethora of examples from individuals within the alternative community seeking to dress like themselves in corporate environments, with examples drawing from Victorian-inspired goth fashion to more colourful 'corporate punk' derived examples.

Ultimately, Chris says he feels more like himself, more congruent and therefore genuine. Alongside this, Chris no longer masks (his ADHD) in nearly all the settings in which he delivers careers guidance. This ability to be himself (unmasked) has developed hand in hand with his being more tattooed.

The psychological aspect of feeling more like himself, and greater congruency, is multilayered. These themes could probably form part of a much longer study exploring this in practice with different practitioners!

We certainly aren't saying 'go and get tattoos, to become a better practitioner' or 'to build greater rapport with clients'! However, reflecting on our own identity, the clothes and symbols we wear, and what this signifies to ourselves and others is a nuanced part of how we form relationships and build connections with our clients.

Taking time to reflect and understand what we need to remain, or become, congruent and mindful is worthwhile.

What do his schools make of his tattoos?

None of Chris' schools has questioned, queried or challenged his choices. Whether this is because he is independent of these establishments (not employed by them) and/or down to the value and quality of his delivery, it is hard to say.

A broader observation is that, certainly, since the Covid-19 pandemic, some schools have taken a more relaxed approach to dress codes, whereas others remain quite firm on visible tattoos. It really is important to check the dress code of the organisation you work for and the settings you visit.

Iconography
Related to this is the sometimes contentious issue of personal items which signify a belief or viewpoint:

- religious jewellery;
- pins, badges or labels which indicate political or organisational viewpoints;
- imagery on T-shirts.

In wearing these, we are sending deliberate messages about our foundations and beliefs, whether it is a pin supporting LGBTQIA+ rights or a religious symbol on a necklace.

As part of training to become career professionals, we are taught to be mindful of our own bias and to do all we can to not project this onto our clients.

Chris has written extensively in the past about the impossibility of being completely impartial.

The Open Partnership Model he developed with his colleagues at CXK leans into this and the importance of practitioners being aware of the drivers behind the questions they ask clients and the point of view from which they practise.

Sharing agendas is part of an open, client-centred practice rooted in transparency of agenda and purpose from the start.

Our affiliations, and iconography which we choose to display, affect our agendas.

 **Insider tip**

Either don't display it, or be transparent about your own agenda.

X

X-rated

Sometimes clients talk about inappropriate things!

> **Authors' note**
>
> Jules was working with a young person who explained they really liked anime. In response to the question 'what do you really like about it?' they answered 'the boobs'. And then asked 'is that wrong?' Because Jules did not really want to start talking about boobs, she simply said 'No, I don't think it's wrong for someone your age, but I also don't think it's something we need to talk about in a Careers Interview – it's very personal and not really relevant to your career plans. Is there someone else in school you could talk to about this if you're worried about it?' A suitable member of staff was identified, permission was given to share and the intervention continued.

Occasionally, clients may have inappropriate expectations of you.

Examples:

- You're the only person who helps me; can we be friends?
- We're both adults – can I take you out for a drink?

Or they may behave inappropriately.

Examples:

- Trying to hug or kiss or touch you.
- Talking about explicit or intimate details (outside of a safeguarding context).

Have some scripts in your toolkit for when clients raise things that are inappropriate or that you simply don't feel you should be discussing.

Reminding yourself, and your clients, about our professional codes of conduct can be really helpful here. Whichever professional body you belong to, make sure you are familiar enough with the ethics of our profession to explain to a client why you don't think something is appropriate.

Y

Yet

Even if you aren't feeling confident YET, you can do this!

> *In a growth mindset, people believe that their most basic abilities can be developed through dedication and hard work – brains and talent are just the starting point. This view creates a love of learning and a resilience that is essential for great accomplishment.*
>
> – Dweck, 2015[1]

We can help ourselves, and our clients, to develop a growth mindset by being mindful of the language we use.

Growth mindset – what to say . . .	Fixed mindset – what not to say . . .
'When you learn how to do a new kind of skill you grow your careers brain'	'Not everyone is good at making choices – just do your best'
If you catch yourself saying *'I'm not a very creative person'* just add the word 'yet' to the end of the sentence	'That's OK, maybe creativity isn't one of your strengths'
'That feeling of decision-making being hard is the feeling of your brain growing'	'Don't worry, you'll get it if you keep trying' If people repeat the same strategies that have previously not worked, they may feel inept and/or lose motivation
'The point isn't to get it all straight away . . . the point is to grow your understanding, bit by bit. What do you want to try next?'	'Good effort. At least you tried' Simply rewarding effort does not develop reflective or critical thinking.

[1] https://www.edweek.org/leadership/opinion-carol-dweck-revisits-the-growth-mindset/2015/09

Z

Zenith

Zenith – the time at which something is most powerful or successful . . . what we might call impact!

Sometimes we do create magic moments. 'Ping' moments!

Hold these moments on behalf of yourself and others – don't dismiss impact.

Reflect on the things you and your client did together to make this happen.

Give them the power they deserve.

Always look for and reflect on impact – that's how we can understand how what we do works. Or not!?

But when something does have particularly great impact, share with the rest of us so we can learn – share on social media, in team meetings, as case studies, in training or write a book! It doesn't matter how you share . . . what matters is that you do share.

A couple of hashtags to look out for if you're up for having a go at sharing:

> #careersimpact
> #SoMuchMoreThanTalkingAboutJobs

If you want to share a bit more privately you can find us both on LinkedIn – we'd love to hear from you!

Recognise the power of career development and celebrate it.

Zero tolerance?

We have the same rights as our clients to feel safe. So, the minute you don't feel safe, just get out. The chapter on *Staying Safe* has some practical suggestions.

However, if a client is unaware they are doing something wrong (and it is not harmful, or an immediate threat), should we adopt a policy of zero tolerance?

> Zero tolerance is a policy of not allowing any violations of a rule or law. Many schools have zero tolerance policies for being late, wearing the wrong uniform, not sitting still, being impolite. . . . And it means that students are punished the first time they break a rule.

If we punish clients for simply getting something wrong, there is likely to be a negligible effect on the undesirable behaviour, and it could affect the client's self-esteem, as well as other unintended consequences of harsh punishments, such as resentment or fear.

For some of our clients – neurodivergent people, for example – these rules often seem arbitrary, unfathomable or unachievable. Try sitting still through a 40-minute careers lesson on CVs if you have ADHD!

So, when you are working in someone else's space:

- Find out what the rules are.
- Flag up if there are any rules you don't expect clients to comply with when they are working with you.
- Explain why.

 Authors' note

Jules prefers clients to say what they are thinking in a group session. She is not a fan of putting your hand up and waiting (after all, this is not good role modelling for the world of work or adult life – young people need to develop conversation skills, learn to contribute appropriately without talking over others, ask questions without fear, and not rely on other people's 'permission' to speak).

So, when a school or college has this rule for other lessons, Jules explains her 'careers rules' and clarifies that participants will be congratulated, not punished, for speaking up.

Zero Tolerance?

Closing thoughts

We decided to start writing books to share what we've learnt with others. Hopefully, our musings have given you:

- food for thought;
- some practical tips;
- somewhere to start when you feel a bit stuck;
- a couple more people in the careers sphere you could trust to reach out to;
- a sense of the joy this profession gives both of us;
- a fun read.

Do get in touch if you have any thoughts, comments, concerns, feedback or amusing anecdotes!

Love as always

Chris and Jules

The Zone

Zone = a region or area set off as distinct from surrounding or adjoining parts.

So this is the section without our usual chit-chat – just loads of explainers and links. The information listed in the *Zone* can also be found in the online resources that accompany this book. To access, scan the QR code or visit the website address given at the start of this book.

AI in the context of career guidance
- https://dmhassociates.org/ai-and-career-guidance-beyond-the-buzzwords/
- https://dmhassociates.org/ai-and-the-future-of-careers-provsion-whats-next/

Alphabet soup
- www.abintegro.com/content/Job%20Seeking%20Terms.pdf
- https://uk.indeed.com/career-advice/career-development/business-acronyms

AAC: Augmentative and alternative communication

ABI: Acquired Brain Injury

ADD, ADHD and AuDHD: Attention Deficit Disorder; Attention Deficit and Hyperactivity Disorder; AuDHD - an unofficial but popular term used to describe individuals who are both autistic and ADHD.

ADL: Activities of daily living

AEN: Additional Education Needs

AGCAS: Association of Graduate Careers Advisory Services

ALN: Additional Learning Needs (Wales)

ALNCo: Additional Learning Needs Coordinator (Wales)

AP: Alternative provision

APD: Auditory Processing Disorder

ASC and ASD: Autistic Spectrum Condition (used currently): Autistic Spectrum Disorder (medical terminology used for describing autism)

ASL: Additional Support for Learning (Scotland)

B2B: Business to Business

B2C: Business to Consumer

BSL: British Sign Language

CAMHS: Child and Adolescent Mental Health Service

CDI: Career Development Institute

CDP: Career Development Professional

CEC: Careers Enterprise Company

CEIAG and IAG: Careers Education, Information, Advice and Guidance; Information, Advice and Guidance

CEO: Chief Executive Officer

CFO: Chief Financial Officer

CHC: Continuing Healthcare

COO: Chief Operating Officer

CP: Cerebral Palsy

CQC: Care Quality Commission

CSW: Communication support worker

CSP: Coordinated Support Plan (Scotland)

DCD: Developmental Coordination Disorder – also known as dyspraxia

DE: Department of Education (Northern Ireland)

DE&I: Diversity, Equity and Inclusion

DfE: Department for Education (England)

DfES: Department for Education and Skills (Wales)

DLA: Disability Living Allowance (England, Northern Ireland and Wales) – a benefit for disabled children and young people up to the age of 16

DP: Direct Payment – a payment made directly to a parent or young person to purchase specific services.

DST: Decision Support Tool – the form that is used by the health worker who does the assessment to see if a person is eligible for NHS Continuing Healthcare.

EHCP: Education, Health and Care Plan (England)

EP: Educational psychologist

ESFA: Education and Skills Funding Agency (England)

FASD: Foetal Alcohol Syndrome Disorder

FTE: Full-Time Equivalent

HI: Hearing Impairment

HR: Human Resources

IDP: Individual Development Plan (Wales)

IEP: Individualised Educational Programme (England and Scotland)

KPI: Key Performance Indicator

LA: Local authority (England, Scotland and Wales)

LAC: Looked After Child – any child who is in the care of the local authority

LSA: Learning Support Assistant

MCA: Mental Capacity Assessment

MSI: Multi-Sensory Impairment

ND: Neurodivergent

NICE: National Institute for Health and Care Excellence

NICEC: National Institute for Career Education and Counselling

OFSTED: Office for Standards in Education, Children's Services and Skills.

PA: Personal Assistant

PD: Physical Disability

PDA: Pathological Demand Avoidance

PEP: Personal Education Plan

PfA: Preparing for Adulthood

PIP: Personal Independence Payment (England, Northern Ireland and Wales) – a benefit paid to disabled adults and young people aged 16 and over.

PRU: Pupil Referral Unit

QA: Quality Assurance

RSD: Rejection Sensitivity Dysphoria

SAAS: Student Awards Agency Scotland

SaLT: Speech and Language Therapist

SE and SSE: Signed English – an exact representation of English where a sign is used alongside every spoken word, including fingerspelling words which don't have an equivalent in BSL, such as 'to' or 'the': Sign Supported English – a way of speaking and signing at the same time, using British Sign Language (BSL) signs for key words while speaking English. SSE signers don't sign every word.

SENCO: Special Educational Needs Coordinator (England)

SEN/D: Special Educational Needs and/or Disability (England and Northern Ireland)

SENDIASS: Special Education Needs and Disability Information, Advice and Support Service (England)

SHANARRI indicators (Scotland): Safe, Healthy, Achieving, Nurtured, Active, Respected, Responsible and Included – a set of eight indicators used to measure a child's wellbeing as part of Getting it Right for Every Child (GIRFEC)

SI: Supported Internship

SLCN: Speech, Language and Communication Needs

SpLD: Specific Learning Disabilities

TA, HLTA and ATA: Teaching Assistant; Higher Level Teaching Assistant: Academic Teaching Assistant

TS: Tourette Syndrome

TSI: Training in Systematic Instruction – the system used by Job Coaches is called TSI. A job coach finds out what work involves and then plans ways to help a young person fulfil these tasks. Support is ongoing until the employee has learnt the job.

Assistive tech and text-to-speech apps

- How to Find and Enjoy Your Computer's Accessibility Settings | Microsoft Windows https://www.microsoft.com/en-us/windows/learning-center/how-to-find-computer-accessibility-settings
- Get started with accessibility features on Mac – Apple Support (UK) https://support.apple.com/en-gb/guide/mac-help/mh35884/mac
- Making Chromebooks accessible for people with disabilities https://www.google.com/chromebook/accessibility/
- https://nasen.org.uk/atminiguide
- https://nasen.org.uk/assistive-technology

Body doubling

- https://www.focusmate.com
- https://www.stylist.co.uk/health/mental-health/what-is-body-doubling-adhd-tool-productivity/763543
- https://procrastination-station.co.uk/whats-body-doubling-all-about

Card sorts – a few examples

- Career Navigator Cards https://creativecareercoaching.org/product/career-navigator-bronze-membership/
- Panjango Top Trumps https://panjango.com/products/panjango-trumps
- Shape of Career Cards https://sunrisecareerguidance.co.uk/shapeofcareercards/
- What's Your Strength https://whatsyourstrength.co.uk

Career Development and Inclusive Practice

- *Career Development and Inclusive Practice*, Jules Benton and Chris Targett https://trotman.co.uk/products/career-development-and-inclusive-practice

Career theories and models

- *Career Development Theories in Practice*, Julia Yates https://trotman.co.uk/products/career-development-theories-in-practice

- *Career Development Theory Handbook*, Liane Hambly https://creativecareercoaching.org/product/career-development-theory-handbook-for-individuals/
- *Creative Career Coaching, Theory into Practice*, Liane Hambly, Ciara Bomford https://creativecareercoaching.org/product/creative-career-coaching-theory-into-practice-2019/
- Career Marcr https://marcr.net/marcr-for-career-professionals/career-theory/career-theories-and-theorists

Careers in careers
- https://resourcefulcareers.aflip.in/careersincareers.html#page/1

CDI
- Code of Ethics – Career Development Institute (thecdi.net) https://www.thecdi.net/about-us/cdi-code-of-ethics
- Resources to support observations and self-reflection: https://www.thecdi.net/CDI/media/Write/Documents/CDI_How_to_Use_the_Recommendations_for_Quality_Assurance_Criteria_Career_Development_Intervention_Observation_or_Self_Reflection.pdf
- *'Careers in Careers – Your Guide to a Career that Changes Lives'* https://resourcefulcareers.aflip.in/careersincareers.html#page/1
- CDI position paper on action planning : www.thecdi.net/CDI/media/Write/Documents/Briefing_Paper_-_Career_Action_Planning-web.pdf?ext=.pdf

Complaints
- CDI https://www.thecdi.net/getmedia/45320a0d-7d12-468a-b55d-f05260e66e63/CDI-Discipline-and-Complaints-Procedure-Updated-October-2023.pdf
- AGCAS https://www.agcas.org.uk/write/MediaUploads/Resources/Quality/ComplaintsandConcernsProcedure.pdf

CXK resources
- Reflective Practice Tool for Careers Practitioners https://www.cxk.org/resources/cxk-reflective-practice-tool-for-careers-practitioners/
- Two examples of 'inclusive' resources from CXK include their Careers Ladder and Post-16 Options posters (found on their website and available for free at: https://www.cxk.org/wp-content/uploads/2022/09/Ladder-Levels-5.pdf and https://www.cxk.org/wp-content/uploads/2022/09/GCSE-Options-Poster.pdf)
- Career mapping https://www.youtube.com/watch?v=4wRaWU6M7Nc

- Quizzes
  A list of free-to-access quizzes can be found here: https://www.cxk.org/blog/career-quizzes
- CXK YouTube channel. E.g. researching university choices: https://www.youtube.com/watch?v=ghonhgpLHBc
- https://www.cxk.org/wp-content/uploads/2023/01/QR-Poster-V2.pdf

Disability
- Disability Rights UK https://www.disabilityrightsuk.org/

Disclosure and barring
England, Northern Ireland and Wales
- Through a Registered Body. https://www.gov.uk/government/organisations/disclosure-and-barring-service/about#registered-bodies
- The service is free for volunteers. https://www.gov.uk/government/publications/disclosure-application-process-for-volunteers
- Guidance about regulated activity with children published by the Department for Education (DfE). https://www.gov.uk/government/publications/keeping-children-safe-in-education--2
- Information about regulated activity with adults is available from the Department of Health (DH). https://www.gov.uk/government/publications/new-disclosure-and-barring-services
- The DBS eligibility tool can be used to determine what type of check a role could be eligible for, as can the eligibility guidance. https://www.gov.uk/find-out-dbs-check https://www.gov.uk/government/collections/dbs-eligibility-guidance
- For sole traders – you can use an umbrella body to submit a cheque on your behalf. https://www.gov.uk/find-dbs-umbrella-body

Scotland
- PVG (Protecting Vulnerable Groups) scheme for people doing regulated work with children and protected adults. https://www.mygov.scot/pvg-scheme/types-of-work-covered-by-pvg

Discrimination and hate crime
- https://www.equalityadvisoryservice.com/
- https://www.report-it.org.uk/home

Equity, Diversity, and Inclusion in Career Development
- *Equity, Diversity, and Inclusion in Career Development*, Ifza Shakoor https://trotman.co.uk/products/equity-diversity-and-inclusion-in-career-development

Group guidance and coaching
- https://www.linkedin.com/pulse/all-group-work-guidance-why-difference-matters-sue-edwards-qifzf/

Imposter Syndrome: Self-doubt, confidence and authenticity
Conversations:

- https://youtube.com/watch?v=Zu1y3aHgmTs&si=PzmGHFo9fzH7F5Lf
- https://youtu.be/sAp-BSglwJc?si=bJr-UCBTCcZFTP75
- https://youtu.be/ZdiaTqOelNo?si=vdssWVpQgkz_waaR

Explainers:

- https://impostorsyndrome.com/articles/10-steps-overcome-impostor/
- https://www.youtube.com/watch?v=h7v-GG3SEWQ

Inherent bias in different search tools
- https://www.technologyreview.com/2018/02/26/3299/meet-the-woman-who-searches-out-search-engines-bias-against-women-and-minorities
- https://time.com/5318918/search-results-engine-google-bias-trusted-sources
- https://brave.com/learn/no-tracking-search-engine
- https://www.sciencedirect.com/science/article/abs/pii/S0736585323001326
- https://nshcs.hee.nhs.uk/about/equality-diversity-and-inclusion/conscious-inclusion/understanding-different-types-of-bias

Learning styles
- https://onlineteaching.umich.edu/articles/the-myth-of-learning-styles/
- https://www.educationalneuroscience.org.uk/resources/neuromyth-or-neurofact/children-have-different-learning-styles
- https://www.quora.com/If-learning-styles-are-a-myth-how-should-teachers-deal-with-a-student-s-preference

Mental capacity
- This video explains the Mental Capacity Act in the context of young people youtu.be/tsthYJV0yig
- For more information: https://www.scie.org.uk/mca/introduction/mental-capacity-act-2005-at-a-glance
- Gillick competency and Fraser guidelines: https://learning.nspcc.org.uk/child-protection-system/gillick-competence-fraser-guidelines

Massive Open Online Courses (MOOCs)
- Here are a couple of examples: https://www.edx.org/ and https://www.mooc.org/

Open Partnership Model (OPM)
- Co-authored by Chris with his colleagues at CXK and published in the June 2014 edition of the CDI's magazine, *Career Matters*. Available digitally for CDI members via the CDI resources online.

Philosophy corner
Ikigai (pronounced 'eeky-guy')
Seeking to find balance and harmony at the intersections of: Passion, Mission, Profession and Vocation or What we love, What the world needs, What we are good at and What we can each be paid for.

The different perspectives for life and career are found where each element crosses over (like a Venn diagram); with the 'sweet spot' where they all overlap with each other.

Eudaimonia
Often seen as the flip side of Hedonism (which is implicit in some discourses regarding 'careers' within Western cultures).

As a concept, Eudaimonia emphasises the idea of seeking fulfilment over excess through living virtuously and meaningfully according to our values, while also rising to whatever our unique potential may be.

Within this there is an acknowledgement that there will be challenges, but that ultimately, an outlook centred on each individual pursuing a moral compass (or living through virtues) rather than living solely through a Hedonistic pleasure principle, is a way to live which leads to greater satisfaction with life and in the end, fulfilment.

Eudaimonia is covered in Aristotle's *Nicomachean Ethics*, which concerns itself with the nature of happiness but, as an idea, it has much deeper roots with Plato and Socrates.

In contemporary research attempts have been made not only to measure Eudaimonia but also compare this with alternative approaches (to happiness), such as Hedonism.

> Modern conceptions of Eudaimonic Wellbeing (EWB) are, on the whole, shaped by literature reviews, critical analyses and empirical examinations of their texts. Coupled with modern research into quality of life and subjective wellbeing (SWB), we have come as far as being able to develop measures for the construct.
>
> EWB is defined by Waterman and colleagues (2010: 41) as:
>
> *'quality of life derived from the development of a person's best potentials and their application in the fulfilment of personally expressive, self-concordant goals'*
>
> (Sheldon, 2002; Waterman, 1990; 2008)

As a 'formula' for Eudaimonia, we can describe it as:

- Know who you truly are + develop your unique potential + use your unique potential to fulfil your life goals

Such broad life goals may be anything from trying to help people through to living in harmony with nature.

In pursuit of Eudaimonia, Socrates encouraged people to ask themselves, and others, what was 'good for their souls' as a way to consider a meaningful life.

Hedonism

In contrast to Eudaimonia, Hedonism is the idea that pleasure is paramount (not to be confused with hedonia which means to experience pleasure).

Hedonism sees the pursuit of pleasure as the guiding force for living one's life – to get the most out of life, all activities in life should be geared towards the pursuit of pleasure alone.

We can consider it akin to the 1980s on steroids! It is linked to maximalism in the sense of celebrating and pursuing abundance, with the idea that more of everything and anything to do with pleasure (pretty much) is best.

It is often (sometimes superficially) linked with excess in contemporary culture; the idea that the more money and stuff we accumulate, the better off we will be and therefore (so the idea goes) we will be winning at life and happy.

However, there is more nuance to Hedonism when we dig into it.

For example:

'Ethical hedonism asserts that pleasure is the highest human value, and pain is valueless. This idea led to the development of utilitarianism, a theory of ethical decision-making that determines what is good and right according to the greatest happiness of the greatest number of people.'[1]

Hedonism is a value or position in life, and therefore can be considered a potential driver for 'career'. In seeking pleasure and avoiding pain, it does, however, sit in contrast to some other beliefs or approaches to life which may place value on pain as part of life; as a way to find balance (within life, death and existence) or even as a way to find meaning.

Consider the athletes who 'work through the pain' to get to their fitness goals, or even the individuals who derive pleasure from pain.

There are also other contrasting philosophical positions and viewpoints which ask proponents to use pain and suffering as a way to find meaning.

Nietzsche considered pain as a catalyst for becoming stronger and overcoming difficulties, particularly if this was combined with purpose.

> *'He who has a why to live for can bear almost any how.'*

An example of this is typified by Viktor Frankl, founder of Logotherapy (a survivor of the concentration camps during the Second World War) who said that although we can't control our circumstances, we can control how we respond to them.

However, for the terminally ill, those with lifelong or life-limiting impairments and/or conditions (and their families who care for them) not all will see pain or suffering as either something which can be overcome or as energy for growth.

In contrast (due to how each of us responds differently to circumstances) some will use their situations as fuel to strive and survive, and in doing so find purpose and meaning.

Michael J Fox has spoken and written extensively about his predisposition to look at challenges, including his Parkinson's disease, through a lens of optimism and humour; and the Foundation he set up to look for a cure.

---

1 *(Driver, 2022). Utilitarianism underpins the principlt*

We wouldn't say at all that Michael is lucky to have Parkinson's disease, but his disposition (or the narrative he presents to the wider world) has shaped how he has used it to find purpose and meaning.

The extent to which this is true, or the nuances around this, may vary. What he is like in private is, respectfully, his own story.

> Such stories aren't limited to celebrity: Carolyn Parry of the Careers Sphere drew our attention to Carl Beech. She says, *'He was diagnosed with early onset Parkinson's and has developed a tapping method which helped him. He has been working with some tech folk to develop a tapping device which is showing some remarkable results not just for Parkinson's but also for those with anxiety, dyslexia (where the words move on the page) and other brain-related conditions. He is driven by impact, not cash.'*

Stoics

When Chris was first starting out in careers, one of his colleagues (a Careers Adviser for most of his life) introduced him to Heraclitus, with a quote that they had pinned up on the upstairs office wall at the Connexions Access Point (CAP).

>It read *'A man's character is his fate – Heraclitus'*

This introduced Chris to a philosopher who came before Socrates and Plato, one who led the way for the Stoics, who believed that how one lived, to what principles and beliefs, affected what one's life will eventually be.

Heraclitus was also one of the first philosophers to explore the idea of looking at the world via a lens of rationality.

Many ideas found in later philosophical approaches within education can be related back to Heraclitus' way of thinking; including how we may encourage clients to consider pursuing open rather than closed mindsets, as part of their character development.

- Which principles do they follow?
- How do we help people consider which career management skills and qualities they wish to grow and pay attention to?

The Stoics themselves were an interesting bunch, an eclectic mixture of thinkers, ranging from former slaves to military leaders. What they all had in common was the desire to live by a set of virtues and, through doing so, find success and fulfilment.

'If, at some point in your life', Marcus Aurelius wrote, *'you should come across anything better than justice, truth, self-control, courage – it must be an extraordinary thing indeed'*.

Seeking a life defined by justice, truth, self-control and courage is the anchors which gave the Stoics (modern and those of the past) their destinies, determination and focus.

- How many of these principles could be applied as career management skills and qualities?

A quote which resonates with some (even as a motto) is 'amor fati' (roughly meaning, 'love your fate'). Sometimes seen as the idea of living consciously in the present, and a recognition that all the things that have happened to each of us (good and bad) have brought us to where we are; from the decisions we make to the unplanned events which happened to us. Therefore, life isn't just about having these things happen to us, but about embracing them. Recognising that we wouldn't be who we are now if these things hadn't happened.

As a philosophical approach, it is quite a bold position to take.

Over the last few years, through social media and platforms such as the Daily Stoic, Stoicism has shifted from being a sometimes misunderstood approach to one which has risen in popularity within an increasingly secular society.

Confucianism

Although arising from a different culture than stoicism, Confucianism also looks at the importance of virtues as a way to live a good life. However, it considers the importance of both the state and family, making reference to a specific moral code. For some scholars, it is a political ideology, for others, a religion, a philosophical position or way of life. It is deeply embedded in many Eastern cultures, with Confucius being seen as a transmitter or amplifier of what was considered 'old knowledge' when he lived.

As a philosophy, it is embedded in reverence for the past and in our ancestors. Benevolent or moral leadership is considered a cornerstone of its approach. It is these other aspects which make Confucianism interesting to us today. There is, perhaps, a kinship to some of the aspects expressed within social justice and the commentaries musing to what extent the state should be involved in how people live, and how to grow a safe society for the good of all within modern life.

It considers aspects of service and is less focused on the individual as the sole arbitrator of considering what is meaningful or worth pursuing in life. Respect for parents and their filial authority is part of this.

Many of us who have been raised within Western cultures can find this difference in philosophical view challenging. Traditional careers guidance (in the West) sees the individual client as the decision maker in their own destiny; whereas in some cultures this isn't the case. Having a broader understanding of these alternative viewpoints can enable us to be more enlightened practitioners.

Confucianism and other philosophical approaches which consider the idea of success or meaning, not just through the lens of the individual and their choices, are useful sources of underpinning knowledge for thought and discussion – providing us with the knowledge and insights to help us understand and appreciate the alternative viewpoints of some of the clients we support.

Clinical and career psychologist, Gideon Arulmani, in recent years has often urged Western career practitioners to consider carefully their assumptions around career choice, guidance and the concept of individual freedom of choice. We need to be respectful of alternative views as we help our clients navigate sometimes conflicting experiences and expectations around what the future may hold. And consider those clients we support who bridge different cultures . . . migrants or international students, for example.

Te Whare Tapa Whā

This is a philosophy from New Zealand which integrates the importance of family and health into career theory. It was developed by Dr Mason Durie in 1982.

Wellbeing (or health) is supported by four pillars (or dimensions) representing *'the basic beliefs of life – te taha hinengaro (psychological health); te taha wairua (spiritual health); te taha tinana (physical health); and te taha whānau (family health)'.*

> *These four dimensions are represented by the four walls of a house. Each wall is necessary to the strength and symmetry of the building.*[2]

Based on the Maori approach to life and family, it sees that building a life (or career) which attends to each of these facets is important; taking a holistic approach. The wharenui (meeting house) of the Maori is a key symbol within this.

---

[2] https://www.careers.govt.nz/resources/career-practice/career-theory-models/te-whare-tapa-wha/

Akin to Confucianism, the whānau (family) can deeply influence the career choices individuals make.

Socratic questioning

This is something which crops up in philosophy 101 but also within basic careers training, teacher training and counselling. Socrates remains the master of the examined life and the art of questioning. Centuries later, his approaches resonate with the work we do each day.

If you haven't considered his influence, reading up on him is worthwhile. Much of what we know of him and his ideas comes from what one of his pupils (Plato) wrote; as he left no written words himself.

What are Socratic questions and what do they have to do with life?

In a nutshell, it is the exploration of a thread . . . the pursuit of a line of questioning, to get to a shared consensus or find meaning. Using open questions and exploring assumptions and bias, by questioning what we consider to be true.

It is an approach which resonates today and has a direct link to careers guidance practice. If you search 'Socratic questioning' or the 'Socratic method' on the internet, you will find plenty to read and even exemplar videos you can watch.

Kaizen

Let's detour to look at a work-focused philosophy which is less about how to live, but rather, focused on how to work.

Kaizen focuses on the idea of making continuous small improvements to daily working practices to build success; from staff wellbeing through to business functions and processes, Kaizen's focus is the pursuit of improvement, just not from the top down.

Everyone in a company is encouraged to consider how they can contribute to the whole. Teamwork and a sense of the greater good are part of the picture.

> *The goal of kaizen is to make small changes over time to drive continuous improvement within a company. The kaizen process recognizes that small changes now can add up to huge impacts in the future. . . . The philosophy is that everyone has a stake in the company's success and everyone should strive, at all times, to help make the business better.*[3]

---

3 https://www.investopedia.com/terms/k/kaizen.asp

Solutions, however, should be viable and lead to efficiencies. The Kaizen Institute, founded by Masaaki Imai, lists the key principles of Kaizen as:

- Know your customer;
- Let it flow (eliminate waste, or non-value-adding activities, from the workflow);
- Go to gemba (where things actually happen, such as the factory floor);
- Empower people;
- Be transparent.

Underlying kaizen is the recognition that the people who perform certain tasks and activities know the most about them. Empowering those people to effect change is the best strategy for improvement.

Sometimes it is seen as a mindset; it is a concept which has travelled round the world and can now be found in many different businesses outside of Japan.

We might consider how this approach could improve daily performance in our own work but also with students struggling in education to help them improve their own outcomes.

- Applying it to things like revision and homework may help our clients to thrive.

Existentialism
Either everything has meaning or nothing does!

Existentialism is the precursor to the post-modern age, representing an enquiry of thought which defined European art and culture within the 19th and 20th centuries. In a nutshell, it contends that life has no inherent meaning, only that which people bring to it or make for themselves. In doing so, people are free to make their own choices but, in turn, are therefore responsible for these choices.

We could say that within an indifferent universe, life is what you make it (or make of it).

There are a variety of views within Existentialism: as a philosophy it is often seen as grounded in atheism. However, there is also theistic existentialism that positions the world as indifferent, but one which is still grounded in God's oversight (Kierkegaard is worth exploring, if this aspect of Existentialism appeals to you).

It can be soul destroying (in a literal sense) as it heads us towards nihilism – but unlike the former, Existentialism says it is down to us to provide life with meaning; the position humanists take.

In this sense, it is a hopeful position unless individuals struggle to find, or fill, life and existence with meaning.

For those with depression and/or other mental health conditions, this can be a real struggle. Being aware of this dimension, while providing careers guidance, matters.

80,000 hours is an organisation which looks at meaning and purpose through the lens of contributing to the social good. They take an analytical approach to careers support, rather than the humanistic careers guidance approaches we are more familiar with.

There is a lot of work being done in the area of how careers work can impact happiness, wellbeing and work-readiness as a way to measure the wider impact of what we do. Take a look at Dierdre Hughes' website (https://dmhassociates.org/) to find out more.

Perhaps we should also consider researching how careers work can help clients find meaning and purpose in a world framed via an existentialist viewpoint?

From a careers guidance viewpoint, following the work of PhD researcher Robin Stevens is worthwhile, as he grapples with Existentialism for Careers in his articles.

There are many different meaningful ways to live. We should reflect on where our own values and judgements land to reduce assumptions which may unduly drive or influence our approaches within careers work.

Use the links below to find out more:

- https://www.bbc.co.uk/worklife/article/20170807-ikigai-a-japanese-concept-to-improve-work-and-life
- https://positivepsychology.com/eudaimonia
- https://medium.com/@MavenDC/he-who-has-a-why-to-live-can-bear-almost-any-how-friedrich-nietzsche-01cb627003dd
- https://www.michaeljfox.org/michaels-story
- https://www.beechband.com/pages/about
- https://positivepsychology.com/hedonism
- https://dailystoic.com/what-is-stoicism-a-definition-3-stoic-exercises-to-get-you-started

- https://dailystoic.com/amor-fati-love-of-fate
- https://modernstoicism.com/heraclitus-and-the-birth-of-the-logos
- https://www.britannica.com/topic/Confucianism
- https://www.researchgate.net/profile/Gideon-Arulmani
- https://thepromisefoundation.org/guiding-principles
- https://careersintheory.wordpress.com/2010/04/15/cultural-beliefs-in-careers-guidance/
- https://www.careers.govt.nz/resources/career-practice/career-theory-models/te-whare-tapa-wha
- https://www.careers.govt.nz/assets/pages/docs/Final-career-theory-model-te-whare-tapa-wha-20170501.pdf
- https://positivepsychology.com/socratic-questioning
- https://www.investopedia.com/terms/k/kaizen.asp
- https://80000hours.org/about
- https://dmhassociates.org/career-development-and-wellbeing-a-focus-on-youth-in-schools
- https://existentialcareers.substack.com
- https://maycontainphilosophy.com/atheistic-and-theistic-existentialism
- https://humanists.uk
- https://medium.com/@lgm527/42-cbcb2773bcab
- https://positivepsychology.com/viktor-frankl-logotherapy

Pre-session information examples
- https://www.cxk.org/services/career-guidance-young-people
- https://www.cosmic-cactus.com/general-7
- Careers (libertygroupltd.co.uk)

Rejection sensitivity dysphoria
- https://neurodivergentinsights.com/rsd-and-friendships/
- https://enna.org/tips-for-communicating-with-those-who-have-rejection-sensitive-dysphoria-rsd/

Role of the careers adviser within 1:1 personal guidance
- www.thecdi.net/CDI/media/Write/Documents/CDI_119-Role_of_a_Careers_Adviser-2021-FINAL_v_to_use.pdf?ext=.pdf

Selective mutism
- https://www.selectivemutism.org.uk/

Short lives
- https://www.togetherforshortlives.org.uk/
- Information on transition https://www.togetherforshortlives.org.uk/changing-lives/developing-services/transition-adult-services/
- Bereavement support, end-of-life planning, and a summary of professional and family publications https://www.togetherforshortlives.org.uk/app/uploads/2021/12/Publication-catalogue_2.pdf

Social model of disability
- https://www.sense.org.uk/about-us/the-social-model-of-disability/

Software and digital tools
- You can see some resources available here – https://www.thecdi.net/resources/digital-resources/software-and-digital-tools-to-support-practice

Staying safe and safeguarding
- https://www.suzylamplugh.org/
- https://www.scie.org.uk/safeguarding/
- https://www.hsqe.co.uk
- https://learning.nspcc.org.uk
- https://www.cpdonline.co.uk

Terry Pratchett
- In 1995 in an interview with Bill Gates for GQ: https://www.theguardian.com/books/2019/may/30/terry-pratchett-predicted-rise-of-fake-news-in-1995-says-biographer

When do we know?
- https://www.youtube.com/watch?v=QLG55zbJIvg

A short video from CXK where Chris explains developmental career theory with the help of a Lego friend.

DISCOVER TROTMAN'S
CAREER DEVELOPMENT INSTITUTE
COLLECTION

The Career Professional's Guide to Research
9781911724599
By Emma Bolger

Equity, Diversity, and Inclusion in Career Development
9781911724698
By Ifza Shakoor

The Career Development Professional's AI Toolkit
9781911724650
By Michael Larbalestier and Marianne Wilson

Sustainable Careers
9781911724537
By Liz Painter

Career Coaching for Midlife and Beyond
9781911724711
By Denise Taylor

The Career Development Professional's Survival Guide
9781911724674
By Jules Benton and Chris Targett

trotman | **t** (Estd. 1969)

Enhance your careers library with careers essentials, free resources and expert articles

Visit www.trotman.co.uk